What's gray, weighs 2,000 pounds, and spins around like a top?
A hippo stuck in a revolving door.

. . . .

How can you tell the difference between a zebra corporal and a zebra sergeant?
The zebra sergeant will have more stripes.

. . . .

ATTENTION: Moles sell houses hole sale.

. . . .

What's black and white and red all over?
A sloppy penguin eating tomato soup.

. . . .

What weighs two tons and is gray and lumpy?
A hippo with the mumps.

. . . .

Why do chameleons make great party guests?
Because they always blend in.

. . . .

Knock! Knock!
Who's there?
I adder.
I adder who?
I adder in a trap, but she escaped.

. . . .

ATTENTION: Wild hogs tell boaring stories.

. . . .

What do you get if you cross an antelope with a journalist?
A gnus reporter.

. . . .

What do you call a seasick rhino?
A green horn.

Knock! Knock!

Who's there?

Gecko.

Gecko who?

Gecko-ing or you'll be late for school.

....

What goes "Bounce! Bonk! Bounce! Bonk! Bounce! Bonk!"?

A kangaroo hopping around in a room with a low ceiling.

....

NOTICE: Rich kangaroos always have deep pockets.

....

What do you get if you cross an Australian animal with a cheerleader?

A kangarooter.

....

Why was the lion dripping wet?

He had a water mane break.

....

What do you call a ram that lives at the top of a mountain?

A hillbilly goat.

Knock! Knock!

Who's there?

Weasel.

Weasel who?

Weasel while you work.

....

What's black and white and slowly turning blue?

A very cold penguin.

....

What does a polar bear wear when his head is cold?
An ice cap.

....

What happens when two zebras crash into each other?

They see stars and stripes.

What kind of sharks live in the desert?

Sand sharks.

What kind of sharks eat lions?

Mane-eaters.

What kind of shark has no friends?

A lone shark.

What sign makes a shark happy?

No fishing.

Why are drowning sharks always left to die?

Because who'd give a shark mouth-to-mouth resuscitation?

What did the shark say when he saw Moby Dick?

I think I'll have some white meat.

What does a shark call a bunch of fish swimming together?

A school lunch.

Why did the great white go to the hospital?

He needed shark therapy.

What do you get when you cross a kangaroo with a jungle vine?

A jump rope.

What do you get if you cross a hyena and a parrot?

An animal that laughs and then asks itself what's so funny.

What do you get if you cross frogs with chameleons?

Leapin' lizards.

What do you get if you cross a hippo with a hog?

The world's biggest pork chops.

What do you get if you cross a sheep and a large primate?
A bah-boon.

What do you call a dapper king of the jungle?

A dandy lion.

What do you get if you cross a coyote and a chimp?
A howler monkey.

What kind of exercises do bunnies do?
Hareobics.

What do you get if you spill boiling water down a rabbit hole?
Hot cross bunnies.

What theory did the famous skunk philosopher propose?
I stink, therefore I am.

THE

SUPER

DUPER

JOKE

BOOK

Volume 1

APPLESAUCE PRESS

KENNEBUNKPORT, MAINE

CONTENTS

CHAPTER 1

KOOKY ANIMAL KINGDOM

Where did the actor skunk deliver his monologue?
Scenter stage.

what do space squirrels like to eat?
Astronuts.

What do you get if you cross minks and pines?
Very expensive fur trees.

What do you get when a bunny marries Bambi?
Hare deer everywhere.

Show me two skunks who enlist in the Marine Corps, and I'll show you a phew good men.

what do you call a grizzly that sheds? Bear naked.

What lives in an oak tree and cooks greasy meals?
A frying squirrel.

How do rabbits fly to Europe?
They take a hare plane.

. . . .

What's soggy and has large antlers?
A rain deer.

. . . .

How much money do a dozen skunks have?
They have twelve scents.

. . . .

How can you tell if a tree is a dogwood?
Check out its bark.

. . . .

What's black and white and green all over?
A sloppy skunk eating pea soup.

. . . .

Why couldn't the herd of deer buy dinner?
Because they only had one buck.

. . . .

What did the judge say when lawyer skunk appeared before him?
Odor in the court.

. . . .

How do you get rid of unwanted rabbits?
Use hare remover.

. . . .

What did Mr. Beaver say to the oak tree?
It's been nice gnawing you.

. . . .

ATTENTION:
Skunks use smell phones.
Snake phones have crawler I.D.
Roadrunner phones have speed dial.

What's the slowest way to send a letter?

Snail mail.

....

Then there was the gopher publisher who printed an underground newspaper.

....

Why was the fox so depressed?

The hunting dogs kept hounding him day and night.

....

Knock! Knock!

Who's there?

I flounder.

I flounder who?

I flounder in the shoe department.

What did Ms. Frog wear on her feet?

Open toad shoes.

....

How did Mr. Turtle pay his bills?

He shelled out cash.

....

What's worse than buying mittens for an octopus?

Buying sneakers for a centipede.

....

Which animal lives in the White House and eats fish?

The presidential seal.

....

What's the best way to save a frog's life?

Clamp his mouth shut so he can't croak.

What did Judge Mole say to the gopher witness?

Remember to tell the hole truth.

Why did the boy porcupine follow the girl porcupine everywhere she went.

He was stuck on her.

Knock! Knock!
Who's there?
Gopher.
Gopher who?
Gopher a walk to calm your nerves.

What kind of bread does a gopher eat?

Hole wheat.

What did one porcupine say to the other.

Quit needling me.

What does Bullwinkle Moose drink when he has an upset stomach?

Elk-o-seltzer.

What do you get if you cross a turtle with a flock of geese?

A slow-down zone.

What did Mrs. Fox say to Baby Fox when she put him to bed?

Pheasant dreams, son.

Quit needling me!

Knock! Knock!
Who's there?
Rabbit.
Rabbit who?
Rabbit up. It's an order to go.

Why was the little bunny in the timeout chair?

He was having a bad hare day.

Mother: Why did you take your goldfish out of the bowl?

Boy: He needs a bath.

. . . .

What do you call a boy slug that lives in a shell?

Snail male.

. . . .

What happened to the frog that parked near a fire hydrant?

He got toad away.

. . . .

What did the robber porcupine say to his quills?

It's time for a stick up.

. . . .

Why did Mr. Mole risk all of his poker chips on one hand?

Because he wanted to gopher broke.

. . . .

Why do rabbits never go bald?

They constantly reproduce hares.

. . . .

How does a skunk get rid of odors?

He uses an ex-stink-guisher.

What is a rabbit's favorite playground game?

Hopscotch.

. . . .

What do rabbits like to eat for dessert?

Carrot cake.

. . . .

What do you call a very athletic hare?

A jock rabbit.

. . . .

Why was the lion king sad and lonely?

He had no pride.

. . . .

What do little frogs use to catch fish?

Tadpoles.

What did the waiter say to the skunk?
May I please take your odor, sir?

◄ ◄ ◄ ◄ ◄ ◄ ◄ ◄ ◄ ◄ ◄ ◄

Do rabbits use combs?
No. They use hare brushes.

◄ ◄ ◄ ◄ ◄ ◄ ◄ ◄ ◄ ◄ ◄ ◄ ◄

NOTICE: Sane squirrels live in nut houses.

► ► ► ► ► ► ► ► ► ► ► ► ► ► ► ► ►

What do you get if you cross a skunk
with a hand grenade?
A stink bomb.

◄ ◄ ◄ ◄ ◄ ◄ ◄ ◄ ◄ ◄ ◄ ◄ ◄ ◄ ◄ ◄ ◄

What kind of stories did Mrs. Rabbit tell her children at bedtime?
Cotton tales.

► ► ► ► ► ► ► ► ► ► ► ► ► ► ► ► ►

ATTENTION: Mr. Frog has a bachelor pad at his pond.

◄ ◄ ◄ ◄ ◄ ◄ ◄ ◄ ◄ ◄ ◄ ◄ ◄ ◄ ◄ ◄

What do you call a moose that tells tall tales?
A bull moose.

► ► ► ► ► ► ► ► ► ► ► ► ► ► ► ► ►

What is a squirrel's favorite Christmas show?
The Nutcracker.

What do you get if you cross a rabbit with morning mist?

Hare dew.

Why did Ms. Bunny go to the beauty parlor?

To get her hare set.

Knock! Knock!
Who's there?
Odor.
Odor who?
Odor men are wiser than younger men.

Knock! Knock!
Who's there?
Distinct.
Distinct who?
Distinct of a skunk is awful.

Which skunk girl went to a fancy ball?

Scenterella.

What do you call a skunk that carves figures out of wood?

A whittle stinker.

What do you get if you cross a hot-air balloon with a skunk?

Something that raises a stink.

What has three ears and a cotton tail?

A rabbit eating corn on the cob.

What do you get if you cross a turtle with a pig?

A trailer pork.

ATTENTION: Turtles are shellfish reptiles.

Why did Bambi fail his test?

His teacher didn't want to pass the buck.

How does a snake navigate through a strange forest?

He uses a GPHiss system.

Knock! Knock!

Who's there?

Possum.

Possum who?

Possum some relish on his hotdog.

You tortoise everything we know

What did the little turtles say to their father?

You tortoise everything we know.

In which direction did the turtle move when he saw us watching him?

Tortoise.

Miss Tortoise: Humph! You're a real square.
Mr. Turtle: What do you expect? I'm a box turtle.

HINKY PINKIES
What do you call ...
A rodent's mate? A mouse spouse.
A tadpole's diary of his travels? A frog log.
A big rodent's rug? A rat mat.
Smokey's recliner? A bear chair.

Tim: Any animal that's not tame is a dangerous creature.
Slim: Now that's a wild accusation.

Marty: Have you ever seen a coyote jog?
Artie: No, but I've seen a fox trot.

What do you get if you cross the U.S. Post Office with Smokey Bear?
I don't know, but it stamps out a lot of forest fires all across the country.

What's black and white with splashes of red?
Two skunks having a rotten tomato fight.

Ranger: I saw a grizzly in a nudist camp.
Guide: Was he bear naked?

What do you get if you cross a rattlesnake with a car tire?
A snake that rattles and rolls.

Then there was the hard-working gopher that built his home business from the ground up.

What is a skunk's favorite holiday?
Scent Valentine's Day.

Mr. Lion: A couple of antelopes just moved into the house next door.
Mrs. Lion: Let's go welcome our gnu neighbors.

Why did Ms. Antelope go to the beauty parlor?
She wanted a gnu hairstyle.

Did you hear about the lions that went out on the town and had a roaring good time?

What do you get if you cross a noisy chimp with a prizefighter? A chatter boxer.

What do monkeys use to make their sandwiches?
Banana bread.

What do you get if you cross a needle and a tiger?
A pin-striped jungle cat.

Knock! Knock!
Who's there?
Hyena.
Hyena who?

Hyena tree sits the majestic eagle.

What time is it when you see a hippo sitting on your doghouse?
Time to get a new doghouse.

Which monkey can fly?
The hot-air baboon.

Mr. Antelope: My wife and I just had a baby.
Mr. Warthog: Congratulations on being gnu parents.

What did the hitting instructor say to the python?
Choke up on your bat.

What do you get if you cross a chimp with a noisy beehive?
Monkey buzzness.

KOOKY QUESTION: Do snow leopards like ice cream?

Knock! Knock!
Who's there?
Lion.
Lion who?
Lion will get you into trouble, so be truthful.

Knock! Knock!
Who's there?
Lion.
Lion who?
Lion on a block of ice can send shivers down your spine.

What's black and white and has red cheeks?
An embarrassed zebra.

ATTENTION:
Some jungle animals have beastly luck.

Knock! Knock!
Who's there?
Thea.
Thea who?
Thea later alligator!

What's black and white and slightly green?
A seasick zebra.

What's hairy and hops up and down?
A gorilla on a pogo stick.

What did Mr. Antelope wear to his wedding?
A gnu suit.

Why was the lion comedian a smash hit in Vegas?
The audience was full of laughing hyenas.

Knock! Knock!

Who's there?

A lioness.

A lioness who?

A lioness king of beasts.

What happens when thousands of lions go to a sporting event?

The crowd really roars.

What do you call a lion that gobbles up your father's sister?

An aunt eater.

What did the boa say to the python?

I have a crush on you.

Lion: Do you want to race me?

Leopard: That depends. You're not a cheetah, are you?

What did the ape say when his sister-in-law had a baby?

Well, I'll be a monkey's uncle!

What did the grapes say when the hippo stepped on them?

Nothing. They just let out a little whine.

What's multi-colored, slithers, and has a forked tongue?

A rainboa.

What do you get if you cross solar flares and a leopard?

Sun spots.

....

Why are chimps awful storytellers?

Because they have no tales to speak of.

....

Where does a lion keep an antelope?

In a prey pen.

....

NOTICE: Then there was the rhino that joined the army and traded in his horn for a bugle.

What are antelopes and gazelles?

Just plain African animals.

....

What did the tiger say to the sailor?

Do you want to be my prey, mate?

....

ATTENTION: Giraffes are heads above other African animals in every respect.

....

Why is it difficult for a giraffe to apologize?

Because it takes a long time for a giraffe to swallow its pride.

....

How does a rhino navigate safely on a misty morning?

He uses his fog horn.

....

ATTENTION: Moles like ground coffee.

....

Knock! Knock!

Who's there?

Woodchuck.

Woodchuck who?

Woodchuck come to our party if we invited him?

DAFFY DEFINITION:

Bat: A mouse with a pilot's license.

....

what did Mr. Squirrel send his girlfriend when he joined the Army?

Forget-me-nuts.

....

Mr. Turtle: What did you buy for Mr. Snake and Ms. Kitty when they got married?

Miss Pooch: Hiss and Purrs bath towels.

....

What do you get if you cross a bison and a duck?

A buffalo bill.

....

NOTICE: Male lions like to live on the African mane land.

....

what do you get when a fast spotted cat falls in a mud puddle?

A dirty cheetah.

....

What does a gorilla wear in the kitchen?

An ape-ron.

Why did the silly rodents always bump into tree trunks?

They were tree blind mice.

....

How does a zebra travel from place to place?

He hoofs it.

....

what do you call a man who rides an elephant?

A trunk driver.

....

What do you get if you cross a rhino with a footwear salesman?

A rhinoceros with a shoehorn.

Which jungle animal is always pouting?
A whinoceros.

. . . .

What do North Pole stockbrokers read?
The Walrus Street Journal.

. . . .

What happens when a skunk crawls through a flower garden?
He ends up smelling like roses.

. . . .

What did the baseball manager say to the boa?
Let's try the squeeze play.

. . . .

What did the baseball umpire say to the sheep?
Ewe are out!

. . . .

Why did the kangaroo infielder miss the ground ball?
Bad bounce.

. . . .

SIGN ON A MOUSEHOLE EXIT: Creep out.

. . . .

Scientist: I just crossed a duck with a bottom-dwelling fish.
Reporter: If your experiment is a success, it'll be a feather in your carp.

. . . .

What do you get when you subtract rabbits from bunnies?
Hare problems.

. . . .

Knock! Knock!
Who's there?
Gibbon.
Gibbon who?
Gibbon is always better than receiving.

Which rodent makes a good baseball shortstop?
A field mouse.

....

Which mink was a barbarian warrior?
Chinchilla the Hun.

....

Knock! Knock!
Who's there?
A rattle.
A rattle who?
A rattle squeal on his friends every time.

....

Hunter: I spotted a leopard.
Guide: Baloney! They're born that way.

....

What did one duck football player say to the other duck football players?
Let's puddle up.

....

How do you bring a rabbit back to life?
Use hare restorer.

....

What did Mr. Rabbit give Miss Bunny?
A 24-carrot ring.

....

GOOFY MATCH GAME
They're a perfect match. She eats like a bird ... and he's a bookworm.
They're a perfect match. She's a real thoroughbred ... and he's mule headed.
They're a perfect match. She's as timid as a mouse ... and he's a sneaky rat.
They're a perfect match. She's a little deer ... and he doesn't have a buck to his name.
They're not a perfect match. She's a cute young kid ... and he's a grumpy old goat.

What does an ill rabbit drink?
Hare tonic.

▶ ▶ ▶ ▶ ▶ ▶ ▶ **KOOKY QUESTION:** Do crocodiles wear alligator shoes?

Are giraffes intelligent?

Yes. They're one of the highest forms of animal life.

What happened when the lioness invited the tiger to dinner?
The tiger ate the lion's share of the food.

What do you call an Asian ox that talks too much? A yakety-yak.

Why do fish like to eat worms?

Who knows! They're just hooked on them.

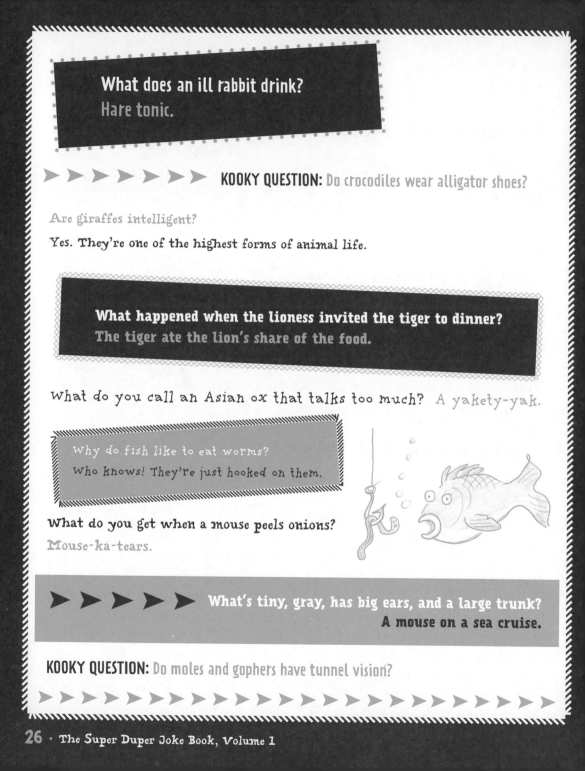

What do you get when a mouse peels onions?

Mouse-ka-tears.

▶ ▶ ▶ ▶ ▶ **What's tiny, gray, has big ears, and a large trunk?**
A mouse on a sea cruise.

KOOKY QUESTION: Do moles and gophers have tunnel vision?

▶ ▶

Why did the kangaroo tourist put a zipper on its pouch?

It was afraid of pickpockets.

Cowboy: I just saw a baby snake.
Cowgirl: How do you know it was a baby?
Cowboy: It had a rattle.

What is a mouse's favorite dessert? Cheesecake.

ANIMAL TONGUE TWISTERS

Lazy Larry Llama loves lovely Lacy Lion.

Timmy Turtle texted Tillie Tortoise ten times.

Hairy Harry Hound hurries home.

Sheep shouldn't sleep in shaky shacks.

Pretty Pinky Porker pines for Porky Peter Pointer.

Ron Watts runs rat races.

How did the beaver break his teeth?
He wandered into a petrified forest.

What animal can jump higher than the Empire State Building?

Any animal. The Empire State Building can't jump.

What do you get if you cross a zebra and a penguin?

An animal in a striped tuxedo.

◄ ◄ ◄ ◄ ◄ ◄ ◄ ◄ ◄ ◄ ◄ ◄

Knock! Knock!

Who's there?

Asp.

Asp who?

Asp your mother if you can come out.

◄ ◄ ◄ ◄ ◄ ◄ ◄ ◄ ◄ ◄ ◄ ◄ ◄ ◄

What do you get if you cross a turtle and an ATM machine?

A creature that shells out cash.

► ► ► ► ► ► ► ► ► ► ► ► ► ► ►

What's the difference between a comedian and a squirrel?

A comedian cracks nutty jokes and a squirrel just cracks nuts.

◄ ◄ ◄ ◄ ◄ ◄ ◄ ◄ ◄ ◄ ◄ ◄ ◄ ◄ ◄

What do you get if you cross a frog and a calendar?

Leap year.

► ► ► ► ► ► ► ► ► ► ► ► ► ► ►

Why was the rabbit with a broken foot so sad?

He had an unhoppy birthday.

◄ ◄ ◄ ◄ ◄ ◄ ◄ ◄ ◄ ◄ ◄ ◄ ◄ ◄ ◄

What do you get if you cross a kangaroo with a pirate?

A sailor who jumps ship.

► ► ► ► ► ► ► ► ► ► ► ► ► ► ►

Todd: A family like yours should be illegal.

Rod: So zoo us.

What has long ears, a bushy tail and chops down trees?
A lumberjack rabbit.

< < < < < < < < < < < < <

What financial advice did Mr. Mole give to Mr. Gopher?

Don't burrow money.

< < < < < < < < < < < < <

what kind of punch does a boxer turtle throw?

A slow poke.

> > > > > > > > > > > >

Why don't they invent:
Bulletproof vests for animals to wear during hunting season?
A GPS device homing pigeons can use?
Miniature cows that give condensed milk?
Feather toupees for bald eagles?
Tiny waterbeds for pet goldfish?

> > > > > > > > > > > > > > > > >

What do you call an Arctic bear that competes in the Olympics?
A polar vaulter.

< < < < < < < < < < < < < < < < <

what do you get if you cross a seal and a cougar?
A sea lion.

> > > > > > > > > > > > > > > > >

When doesn't a skunk smell?
When its nose is clogged up.

Who has lots of long arms and is a Western outlaw?
Billy the Squid.

What do you get if you cross a Christmas plant with a female deer?
Mistle-doe.

WHAT A WILD NEIGHBORHOOD!
My big brother belongs to the Elks Club.
My father is a member of the Moose Lodge.
My uncle belongs to the Lions Club.
My cousin is a card shark.
My little brother is a weasel.
My grandfather is a real turkey.
My grandmother is an old crow.

What's the worst thing a giraffe can have?
Whiplash.

What is a turtle's favorite game?
The old shell game.

What did Mrs. Skunk say to Mr. Skunk at dinnertime?
Can we odor out tonight?

What do you get if you cross large rodents with small, juicy fruits?
A ratsberry bush.

What did Mr. Turtle say to Miss Tortoise?
Shell we dance?

What happens when silk worms race?
They usually end up in a tie.

Animal trainer #1: **How's the giraffe business?**
Animal trainer #2: **Things are looking up.**

Which monkey can't keep a secret?
The blahboon.

blah blah
blah
blah blah

What do you get if you cross an octopus with a piece of furniture?

An arm, arm, arm, arm, arm, arm, arm, armchair.

What takes tons of wool and years to knit?

A turtleneck sweater for a giraffe.

Instructions on a roadrunner's phone: "Please leave your message after the beep, beep!"

What do you get if you cross a small rodent with an oil can?
A mouse that never squeaks again.

Visitor on safari: **Gulp! I'm seeing spots before my eyes.**
Guide: **Relax. That's just a leopard.**

NOTICE: Hippos often sleep in river beds. ◄ ◄ ◄ ◄ ◄ ◄

What do you get if you cross a centipede with a piece of furniture?

A foot, foot, foot, foot stool.

CHATTER CHUCKLES

You tell 'em Monkey ... you're a chimp off the ol' block.

You tell 'em Little Chimp ... you're no cheetah.

You tell 'em Alligator...you're tale is no croc.

Knock! Knock!

Who's there?

Whale.

Whale who?

Whale I guess I'll be going now.

What exercise do you get when you cross kangaroos with athletes?

Jumping jocks.

What do you call a turtle soldier?

A helmet with legs.

What did the kangaroo say to the hitchhiker?

Hop in!

Why did the little piggy stay home?

His room was a pigsty and his mother made him clean it.

Why do leopards wear spotted coats?

The tigers bought all the striped ones.

Where do lions bathe?
In the mane stream.

What happens when two frogs try to catch the same bug at the same time?
They end up tongue-tied.

Knock! Knock!
Who's there?
Gopher.
Gopher who?
Gopher a snack while the commercial's on.

Why did the pig athlete go to the trainer?
He hurt his hamstring.

Why did the pig go to the optometrist?
He had pink eye.

Why did the pig farmer call the vet?
He wanted her to cure his ham.

How did the turtle travel to the Orient?
He took a slow boat to China.

Where does a juvenile delinquent fish swim?
In a reform school.

How did the squid get downtown?
It took an octobus.

Elephants

What did Tarzan say when he saw three elephants wearing sunglasses?
Nothing. He didn't recognize them.

What kind of elephant lives in New Delhi?
An Indian elephant.

What weighs two tons, has a trunk, and loves pepperoni pizza?
An Italian elephant.

ATTENTION: An elephant is a nosy animal.

What's gray, carries flowers, and visits sick people?
A get wellephant.

What did the label on the back of the elephant's designer jeans read?
Wide load.

Why did the elephant have lots of tiny holes in his nose?
He forgot to put mothballs in his trunk.

What do you get if you cross an elephant with a vacuum?
Something that sucks up a lot of dirt.

What did the polite elephant on the subway do?
He stood up and let five ladies take his seat.

What do you get if you cross a steer and a pachyderm?
A bull elephant.

Where's the best place to watch an elephant pole vault?
As far away from the landing pit as possible.

What do you get if you cross an elephant with a shotgun?
A pachyderm with a double barrel trunk.

How did the elephant get his trunk stuck in the drainpipe?
He put his nose where it didn't belong.

What do you get if you cross a bloodhound and a pachyderm?
An elephant with a trunk that can track any scent in the world.

How do you pick up an elephant?
Tell her she's cute and offer to buy her lunch.

What's gray, weighs two tons, and has two wheels?
An elephant on a motorcycle.

Girl: Did Noah take any suitcases on the Ark?
Boy: No. But the elephants brought along two trunks.

What did the peanut vendor say to the elephant?
Keep your nose out of my business.

Boy: Are peanuts fattening?

Girl: Have you ever seen a skinny elephant?

....

Why do cowboys ride horses instead of elephants?

Elephants take too long to saddle.

....

Why do cowboys tame wild horses, but not wild elephants?

Would you want to ride a bucking elephant?

....

What do elephants bring to a sauna bath?

Swimming trunks.

....

What's gray, has big ears, and is ten feet tall?

A mouse on stilts.

....

What did Detective Elephant do at the crime scene?

He nosed around looking for clues.

....

Why didn't Mr. Elephant get rich?

He always agreed to work for peanuts.

....

What do you get if you cross a woodpecker and an elephant?

Something that pecks holes in giant Redwood trees.

....

What does an elephant need to pull heavy loads?

A tow trunk.

....

What has red lips, three tongues, and a trunk?

A girl elephant wearing lipstick and sneakers.

What is an elephant's motto?
Keep on trunkin'.

What's blue, has big ears, and weighs two tons?

A spoiled elephant holding its breath.

. . . .

Why do elephants have white tusks?

They brush after every meal.

. . . .

Knock! Knock!

Who's there?

Harry.

Harry who?

Harry up. I don't want to miss the elephant parade.

. . . .

How do you make a gray elephant blue?

Tell him a sad story.

. . . .

How do you can an elephant?

Just say, "You're fired!"

. . . .

How do you can pink elephants?

Hand them pink slips.

. . . .

What weighs two tons and has a million red dots on it?

An elephant with the measles.

How do you make an elephant float?

Throw him a very big life preserver.

. . . .

Man: I used to have a pet elephant, but I had to get rid of him.

Guy: Why?

Man: I was spending too much time cleaning out the litter box.

. . . .

Why did the elephant fail his Army physical?

He had flat feet.

. . . .

How did the elephant plastic surgeon get rich?

He performed thousands of nose jobs.

Why was the sailor elephant so sad?

His trunk was lost during a storm at sea.

....

What do you get if you cross pachyderms with tiny insects?

Eleph-ants.

....

What do you get if you cross an elephant and a turtle?

I don't know, but you should see the size of its shell.

....

Knock! Knock!

Who's there?

Howell.

Howell who?

Howell I feed my pet elephant?

....

Knock! Knock!

Who's there?

Dozen.

Dozen who?

Dozen anyone want to see the circus elephants?

....

Why are elephants so smart?

They have tons of gray matter.

....

What do you get when an elephant steps on a can of corn?

Creamed corn.

....

What's as big as an elephant, looks like an elephant, but doesn't weigh an ounce?

An elephant's shadow.

How did an elephant get stuck in a tree?
His parachute got caught.

....

Why did the elephant become a reporter?
He had an uncanny nose for news.

....

How can you tell if an elephant is snobby?
A snobby elephant walks around with its nose stuck up in the air.

....

How do you know when an invisible elephant is behind you?
You'll smell the peanuts on his breath.

....

What makes an elephant feel sick?
A pachygerm.

....

Why did the elephant miss his flight to Europe?
Because they took too long searching his trunk at the airport.

....

What has a trunk, weighs two tons, and is red all over?
An elephant with a bad sunburn.

....

What climbs trees, buries nuts, and weighs two tons?
An elephant who thinks he's a squirrel.

....

why did the little elephant spend two hours in the bathtub?
His mother ordered him to wash behind his ears.

Why do elephants make fantastic reporters?
They have a great nose for news.

Why was the boy elephant mad at his date?
She took too long to powder her nose.

Why didn't the elephant tip the bellboy?
Because he dented his trunk.

What do you get if you cross an elephant with an octopus?
An animal that has trunks everywhere.

What do you get if you cross a prehistoric elephant and a flock of sheep?
A very woolly mammoth.

What weighs two tons and plays baseball? A Cleveland Indian Elephant.

What's gray, has big ears, and weighs 500 pounds?
A very obese mouse.

What has a glove compartment and two trunks?
A car being driven by an elephant.

What lives in the jungle, has spots, and weighs two tons?
An elephant with the measles.

What do you get if you cross a centipede and an elephant?
You get out of the way!

Why do elephants have trunks?
Because they'd look ridiculous with suitcases on their faces.

What do you get if you cross a pachyderm with Rudolph the Red-Nosed Reindeer?
An elephant with a trunk that glows in the dark.

Knock! Knock!
Who's there?
Ella.
Ella who?
Ellaphant.

Why do elephants have squinting eyes? From reading the small print on peanut packages.

A man took his trained elephant to the circus. "Dance," he said as the band began to play. Instantly, the elephant began to dance around as the owner of the circus watched closely. When the number ended, the trainer turned to the circus owner. "Well," he said, "are we hired?" "No," replied the circus owner. The trainer was stunned. "Why not?" he asked. "Because," the circus owner snapped, "the band played a waltz and your elephant did a mamba."

Why did the herd of elephants get a ticket?
Because their tail lights didn't work.

What do elephants use bowling balls for? To play marbles.

Why were the elephants the last animals to board Noah's ark?
Because it took them a long time to pack their trunks.

➤ ➤ ➤ ➤ ➤ ➤ ➤ ➤ ➤ ➤ ➤ ➤ ➤ ➤ ➤ ➤ ➤ ➤ ➤ ➤

What do you get if you cross an elephant with an anteater?
The world's best and fastest bug exterminator.

◀ ◀ ◀ ◀ ◀ ◀ ◀ ◀ ◀ ◀ ◀ ◀ ◀ ◀ ◀ ◀ ◀ ◀ ◀ ◀

Barry: **Why do elephants paint themselves purple?**
Larry: **I don't know.**
Barry: **So they can hide on grapevines.**
Larry: **I've never seen an elephant on a grapevine.**
Barry: **That's because they do such a good job.**

➤ ➤ ➤ ➤ ➤ ➤ ➤ ➤ ➤ ➤ ➤ ➤ ➤ ➤ ➤ ➤ ➤ ➤ ➤ ➤

Ike: I went on safari in Africa and late one night I shot an elephant in my pajamas.
Spike: Don't be ridiculous! How could an elephant fit in your pajamas?

◀ ◀ ◀ ◀ ◀ ◀ ◀ ◀ ◀ ◀ ◀ ◀ ◀ ◀ ◀ ◀ ◀ ◀ ◀ ◀

Why do elephants have unlimited credit?
No one is brave enough to stop them from charging.

➤ ➤ ➤ ➤ ➤ ➤ ➤ ➤ ➤ ➤ ➤ ➤ ➤ ➤ ➤ ➤ ➤ ➤ ➤ ➤

What do you get if you cross an elephant and a cornfield?
Giant ears of corn.

◀ ◀ ◀ ◀ ◀ ◀ ◀ ◀ ◀ ◀ ◀ ◀ ◀ ◀ ◀ ◀ ◀ ◀ ◀ ◀

Do elephant musicians read sheet music?
No. They play by ear.

➤ ➤ ➤ ➤ ➤ ➤ ➤ ➤ ➤ ➤ ➤ ➤ ➤ ➤ ➤ ➤ ➤ ➤ ➤ ➤

Elephant: Was that an earthquake? I feel tremors.
Rhino: No. It's just the hippos playing leapfrog.

◀ ◀ ◀ ◀ ◀ ◀ ◀ ◀ ◀ ◀ ◀ ◀ ◀ ◀ ◀ ◀ ◀ ◀ ◀ ◀

What do elephants wear on the beach?
Bathing trunks.

➤ ➤ ➤ ➤ ➤ ➤ ➤ ➤ ➤ ➤ ➤ ➤ ➤ ➤ ➤ ➤ ➤ ➤ ➤ ➤

What do you get if you cross an elephant with a mouse?
I don't know, but it makes big holes in the wall.

Absurdaphants ▶▶▶▶▶▶▶▶▶▶▶▶▶▶▶

Of all the animal jokes out there, why are elephant jokes the silliest? For example:

Why did the elephant wear blue tennis shoes?
Because his white ones always got dirty.

While some elephant jokes are puns or word play (including many in this section), the craziest ones put elephants in situations we don't normally think of them in. The question above is silly because we know elephants don't wear shoes. The answer is funny because not only doesn't it answer the question as to why the elephant is wearing shoes in the first place, but it says the elephant has white tennis shoes, too! It's impossible, absurd, and it makes us laugh! These sorts of elephant jokes have been popular for nearly fifty years, and thankfully, elephants have a good sense of humor, because these jokes are fun to tell and even more fun to come up with. Here are some more. After reading them, try making up some of your own.

How do you get an elephant in the refrigerator?
Open the door, put in the elephant, and then close the door.

How do you know there's an elephant in the refrigerator?
Footprints in the peanut butter.

How do you know there are two elephants in the refrigerator?
You hear giggling when you close the door.

How can you tell when an elephant is hiding in your closet?
You won't be able to get the door shut.

What's gray and bounces?
An elephant on a trampoline.

What's gray, weighs 2,000 pounds, and floats?
An elephant wearing a life jacket.

What has two wheels, giant ears, and wobbles?
An elephant learning to ride a bike.

Can elephants fly?
Yes. But only if they have a pilot's license.

How do you make an elephant float?
Pour soda into a glass, add a scoop of ice cream, and dump in an elephant.

For the Birds

What do you get if you cross two blobs of raw pastry and an ostrich?
A dough-dough bird.

....

What do geese do when they get caught in a traffic jam?
They honk a lot.

....

Who do you get if you cross a water fowl with a Western hero of the O.K. Corral?
Duck Holiday.

....

Why didn't the nervous rooster cross the road?
Down deep he really was really a chicken.

....

What do you get if you cross an eagle and a minister?
A bird of pray.

....

What do you get if you cross pigeons in a coop with pigs?
Roost pork.

....

What do you get if you cross a stork with Sasquatch?
A bird that stands on one big foot.

....

What do you get if you cross a rooster with a parrot?
A bird that yells, "Get up!" at the crack of dawn.

Society Sue: My pet canary is so spoiled she refuses to sing unless she's accompanied by a pianist.

Snobby Robbie: My pet dog is so spoiled, when I command him to sit, our butler has to pull out a chair for him.

. . . .

What did Ms. Flamingo say to Mr. Crane?

Quit storking me.

. . . .

What do you get if you cross a centipede with a myna bird?

A walkie-talkie.

. . . .

Why couldn't Mr. Goose buy a house?

He didn't have a down payment.

. . . .

Which bird skydives out of airplanes?

The parrot trooper.

. . . .

Hen: I don't have much of a nest egg.

Duck: Why is that?

Hen: Because all of my life I've worked for chicken feed.

. . . .

What does a bird maid use to keep the nest clean?

A feather duster.

. . . .

What do crows use to make their sandwiches?

Corn bread.

. . . .

What did the mallard wear to his wedding?

A duckcedo.

Then there was the owl who became a mystery writer and penned several who-done-its.

What happens when pigeons have a hot coop?
They roost themselves.

NOTICE: Acme Bird Phones—We tweet you right!

What did the duck feathers say to the goose feathers?
It's down time at last.

Ollie: I'm a wise old owl.
Robin: So, who gives a hoot?

Knock! Knock!
Who's there?
Owl.
Owl who?
Owl be back in a minute.

DAFFY DEFINITION:
Bird nest: Cheep housing.

How does a crow know who's trying to contact him?
He checks his cawler I.D.

What do you get if you cross a pigeon with a bat?
A bird that roosts upside-down.

What do you get if you cross a rhino with a goose?
A bird with a horn to honk.

What do you get if you cross an owl and a coyote?
A hoot and howler.

What do you get if you cross a coyote with a rooster?
A canine that crows at daybreak or a bird that howls when the moon rises.

Knock! Knock!
Who's there?
Ammonia.
Ammonia who?
Ammonia bird in a cage.

What kind of bird insults people?
A mockingbird.

Where did the little bird go after elementary school?
To junior fly school.

Why was Mr. Duck upset?
His bill was in the mail.

What did Ms. Duck get after her nose job?
A big medical bill.

What game do mother hens play with their chicks?
Peck a boo.

NOTICE: Buy a duck feather phone and get free downloads.

Which bird works at the construction site?
The crane.

What birds work underground.
Coal mynas.

Which owl has a band of merry men?
Robin Hoot.

Mr. Pigeon: I need to go out tonight.
Mrs. Pigeon: Why?
Mr. Pigeon: I've been cooped up at home all week.

How do you post a canary?
Use bird class mail.

What has feathers and holds up banks?
A robber ducky.

What do you call a couple of keets?
Parakeets.

Knock! Knock!
Who's there?
Wottle.
Wottle who?
"Wottle I do now?" asked the turkey.

What do you get if you cross a tortoise and a pigeon?
A turtle dove.

What do you get if you cross wooden shoes with song birds?

Dutch tweets.

What do you get if you cross ducks with popcorn?

Quacker Jacks.

What do you call a baby bird?
A chirp off the old block.

Mr. Duck: **Are those new feathers?**
Mr. Goose: **No. It's hand-me-down.**

What do you call an in air collision between two birds?
A feather bender.

What two birds are in the story of Alice in Wonderland?

Tweeter Dee and Tweeter Dum.

What's black and white and red on the bottom?

A baby penguin with diaper rash.

NOTICE: **Birds snack on potato chirps.**

Worm #1: What's the best way to avoid getting eaten by an early bird?
Worm #2: Sleep late.

What do you get if you cross a canary with a chimp?

A chirp monk.

Knock! Knock!
Who's there?
Egos.
Egos who?
Egos are big birds with keen eye-sight.

....

Knock! Knock!
Who's there?
Who?
Who Who?
What are you, some kind of owl?

....

When does a black bird seek psychiatric help?
When it's a raven maniac.

Who?

....

Where do adult birds go for a friendly drink?
A crow bar.

....

What do you get when you clone a duck and cross the results with a hoagie?
A double ducker sandwich.

What do you get if you cross a tall pink bird with a roadrunner?
A flamingo-go-go.

....

Knock! Knock!
Who's there?
Hens.
Hens who?
Hens up! We've got you surrounded.

....

What do you call a wacky chicken?
A cuckoo cluck.

....

Knock! Knock!
Who's there?
A bird talon.
A bird talon who?
A bird talon fibs is a serious matter.

....

Knock! Knock!
Who's there?
Wren.
Wren who?
Wren in Rome, do as the Romans do.

....

How did the goose earn a free vacation?
He accumulated a lot of frequent flyer miles.

....

Which bird was a star baseball player?
Chirper Jones.

....

Who has feathers and won the lottery?
The Lucky Duck.

DAFFY DEFINITIONS:
Condor: A prison entrance.
Goblet: A baby turkey.

....

Knock! Knock!
Who's there?
Robin.
Robin who?
Robin people is a crime.

....

Mr. Toucan: **Who are those two old birds?**
Mrs. Toucan: **They're my grand-parrots.**

....

What does a 300-pound parrot say?

Polly wants a cracker—so move it!

....

Who has feathers and is a basketball star?

Larry Birdie.

....

Mr. Vulture: **What's for dinner?**
Mrs. Vulture: **Leftovers.**

....

Mr. Vulture: **What would you like to order for dinner?**
Mrs. Vulture: **I'm not hungry. I'll just peck.**

Knock! Knock!
Who's there?
Wren.
Wren who?
Wren you're smiling, the whole world smiles with you.

....

Knock! knock!
Who's there?
N-M-T
N-M-T who?
N-M-T nest makes a mother bird sad.

....

What has feathers and plays jazz music?
A Ducksey—Land Band.

Mr. Goose: **You talk crazy.**
Mr. Duck: **That's why they call me Wild Bill.**

....

Why did Mr. Duck have a lot of mouths to feed?

He was a bill collector.

What did the old tree say to the sapsucker?
Quick pecking on me.

Jack: Why are those storks flying so fast?
Mack: Maybe they're hurry cranes.

ATTENTION: A hen that invests wisely will always have a secure nest egg.

What happened to the flock of geese that landed in a hot spring?
They cooked their own gooses.

Where do pelicans shop for food?
At the fish market.

What has webbed feet and carries a gun?
A duck hunter.

Larry: I named my pet parrot Paulie.
Barry: Paulie want a cracker?

Mr. Goose: **Dr. Duck, I think you're a quack physician.**

Why do baby birds squawk a lot at mealtime?
You'd squawk too if your mother fed you bugs and worms.

What do you get if you cross a gopher and a robin?
A miner bird.

What do you get if you cross owls and mixed breed mutts?
Who curs?

What do you get when geese fly headfirst into a brick wall?
Goose bumps.

What do you get if you cross a magician and a canary?
A trick or tweeter.

What do you get if you cross a mime with duck feathers?
Quiet down.

What kind of pie can fly?
A magpie.

What do you get when you cross a crow with dynamite?
Caw-boom!

What does an owl say when its caller ID isn't working?
Who's calling?

What did the crow say when he saw three ears of corn?
Humm ... which one should I peck?

Horsey Ha Ha's

Which horses wear military uniforms?
Pony soldiers.

. . . .

What did the racehorse say when the temperature reached 100 degrees?
I'm too hot to trot.

. . . .

DAFFY DEFINITION:
Zebra: A horse in a pinstripe suit.

. . . .

How can you prove a horse has six legs?
First count his back legs and then count his fore legs.

. . . .

What do you call a herd of camels packed tightly together?
Humper to humper traffic.

. . . .

Knock! Knock!
Who's there?
Cayuse.
Cayuse who?
Cayuse your bathroom? I gotta go.

. . . .

What does a pony put on his deli sandwich?
Horseradish.

. . . .

What do you get if you cross a giraffe with a thoroughbred horse?
Something that wins a lot of races by a neck.

How can you make a slow racehorse fast?
Stop feeding him.

....

Farmer: How is my sick horse?
Vet: He's in stable condition.

....

Why are horses bad dancers?
They have two left feet.

....

What do you call a male deer and a wild horse standing side by side?
A buck and bronco.

....

What's the quickest way to ship a small horse?
Use pony express.

....

Then there were the newlywed horses that checked into the bridle suite.

....

Mack: I heard you wrote a book about how to stop a stampede of wild horses.
Zack: Yes. It's a tale of whoa.

....

What do you call a vet with laryngitis?
A hoarse doctor.

....

What did the racehorse say to the stable?
Is my fodder in there?

....

DAFFY DEFINITION:
Centaur: a man with good horse sense.

DAFFY DEFINITION:
Thoroughbred racehorse: a barn athlete.

▶ ▶

Billy: When your young thoroughbred colt grows into a horse, are you going to race him?
Willy: Heck no! He's already faster than I am.

◀ ◀

SIGN ON A STABLE: We rent mules and donkeys, but we refuse to give kickbacks to our patrons.

▶ ▶

Tim: Pegasus is a flying stallion with wings.
Jim: That's a lot of horse feathers.

◀ ◀

Knock! Knock!
Who's there?
Mare E.
Mare E. who?
Mare E. Christmas everyone!

▶ ▶

What do you call a camel locked in a famous church in France?
The humpback of Notre Dame.

◀ ◀

ATTENTION: Camels have a dry sense of humor.

▶ ▶

Horse: Don't look so sad, Bronco.
Bronco: Okay. I'll try to buck up.

◀ ◀

SIGN ON A HORSE FARM: America needs a more stable economy.

It's Raining Cats & Dogs

What kind of work does a weary cat do?

Light mousework.

<<<<<<<<<<<<<<<<<<<<

Which holiday do dogs like best?

Howl-o-ween.

>>>>>>>>>>>>>>>>>>>>

Bob: Look. That dog is chasing his tail.
Rob: He's having trouble making ends meet.

<<<<<<<<<<<<<<<<<<<<

ATTENTION: Our neighborhood is so bad our watchdog has a burglar alarm on his dog house.

>>>>>>>>>>>>>>>>>>>>

Which state has the most cats and dogs?

Petsylvania.

<<<<<<<<<<<<<<<<<<<<

What do you get if you cross a poodle and a guppy?

A dog fish.

>>>>>>>>>>>>>>>>>>>>

What do you call a cat that casts spells?

A magic kit.

<<<<<<<<<<<<<<<<<<<<

Don: Can I take a picture of your dog doing a trick?
Ron: Sure. Spike will gladly be a roll model.

What do you get if you cross a barking dog and the ocean?
Ruff Seas.

What did one cat neighbor say to the other?
Our neighborhood is going to the dogs.

Our neighborhood is going to the dogs!

Zack: What do you do when you take your pet dog for an automobile ride?

Mack: We put him in a cur seat.

Why did the pooch go into the clothing store?

He wanted to buy a houndstooth jacket.

Which dog marks test papers?
The Grade Dane.

What did the cowboy say to the two toy poodles sitting before him?
Get along little doggies.

Judy: Where are you going in such a rush?
Rudy: I'm running away from trouble.
Judy: You can't run away from trouble. You have to face it.
Rudy: You face him. Trouble is the name of our neighbor's pit bull and here he comes!

Knock! Knock!
Who's there?
Ken L.
Ken L. who?
Ken L.s are dog hotels.

Knock! Knock!
Who's there?
Tabby.
Tabby who?
Tabby or not tabby, that is the question.

What do you get if you cross spirits with mixed breed dogs?
No body curs.

Boy to Girl: My pet dog is so sophisticated he doesn't speak. He recites poetry instead.

ATTENTION: K9 police make dog collars.

Why do cats climb trees?
Because they don't know how to use ladders.

Knock! Knock!
Who's there?
Irish.
Irish who?
Irish your dog would stop barking.

What is the theme song of the president's dog?
Heel to the Chief.

What do you get if you cross a cantaloupe and Lassie?
A melon-collie dog.

Knock! Knock!
Who's there?
Coincide.
Coincide who?
Coincide and let the dog out.

SIGN ON AN ITCHY DOG: Welcome to the Land of the Flea.

Boy: My dog is a police dog.
Girl: He doesn't look like one.
Boy: He's undercover.

What do you get if you cross a fishing rod with a kitten?
A pole cat.

Why did the cat buy a computer?
So it could play with the mouse.

What do you get if you cross a kitten with crushed tomatoes?
Catsup.

What kind of dogs do angels keep as pets?
Saint Bernards.

What do you get if you cross a dog with a boomerang?
A pet that runs away, but always comes back.

Knock! Knock!
Who's there?
Sheena.
Sheena who?
Sheena lost dog around here?

How can you tell if a cat burglar has been in your house?
Your cat will be missing.

Jim: **My pet hound used to be a great hunting dog.**
Tim: **What happened?**
Jim: **Someone told him it's impolite to point.**

Lady: I like this little dog, but I think his legs are too short.
Pet Store Clerk: They're not too short. They all reach the floor, don't they?

First Dog: Bark! Bark!
Second Dog: Meow! Meow!
First Dog: What's wrong with you? A dog doesn't say "meow!"
Second Dog: I'm learning a foreign language.

Knock! Knock!
Who's there?
Noah kitten.
Noah kitten who?
Noah kitten who wants to play with me?

What kind of pet does the Abominable Snowman have?

A chilly dog.

....

What do you get if you cross a hungry cat and a canary?

A cat that's no longer hungry.

....

Show me a snow leopard ... and I'll show you a real cool cat.

....

Ken: Your dog has a loud, scary bark.

Len: Yup. It sure is a big, bad woof.

....

What dog lives at a baseball stadium?

The catcher's mutt.

....

Knock! Knock!

Who's there?

Design.

Design who?

Design said beware of dog!

....

What do you call mail sent to female cats?

Kitty letter.

....

What kind of car has a motor that purrs?

A catillac.

Girl: Have you ever seen a catfish?

Boy: No. But I've seen a hunting dog.

....

What does a kitten use to part its fur?

A catacomb.

....

What did one itchy dog say to the other?

You scratch my back and I'll scratch yours.

....

When is it bad luck to have a black cat cross your path?

When you're a mouse.

....

ATTENTION: **All young cats must swim in the kitty pool.**

....

Why did Miss Kitty and Mr. Tom Cat get married?

They were a purrfect match.

WANTED: Trained cat to work with bird act. Must know how to keep mouth shut.

....

Knock! Knock!
Who's there?
Kit.
Kit who?
Kit busy and stop asking silly questions.

....

What does a cat put on a hot dog?
Moustard.

....

What do you get if you cross a lemon tree and a cat?

A sour puss.

....

what happens when a watchdog eats garlic?

His bark becomes worse than his bite.

....

What do you get if you cross a canine with a skunk?

A Scent Bernard.

....

Mack: How did your dog break his front paws?

Zack: He did it burying a bone.

Mack: Really? Where?

Zack: In a parking lot.

NOTICE: Then there was the sheepdog that got into trouble for crying "woof" all the time.

Girl: why is your pet dog lying outside your front door?

Boy: He's our welcome mutt.

....

When is a bloodhound dumb?
When he has no scents.

....

What did the weary watchdog say to his master?

I'm tired of you making me sic.

....

Mother: Our new pet dog can't sleep in the house tonight.

Boy: But we haven't finished building his doghouse.

Mother: Well go out and buy him a pup tent.

DAFFY DEFINITION:
Greyhound: A stock cur racer.

....

They're a perfect match ... he's a watchdog and she has lots of ticks.

....

What did the French chef say to his pet pooch at meal time?
Bone appétit!

....

Knock! Knock!
Who's there?
Ty.
Ty who?
Ty up the dog before he runs away.

....

Knock! Knock!
Who's there?
Annette.
Annette who?
Annette is used to catch stray dogs.

....

What do you get if you cross a keg of black powder and a mixed breed dog?
Dynomutt.

....

What do you get if you cross a chili pepper, a gopher, and a pooch?
A hot diggity dog.

....

What do you get if you cross a cat and a cobbler?
Puss in boots.

Why was the little kitten so irritable?
She needed a cat nap.

....

Which feline always enters a room after a drum roll?
The tom-tom cat.

....

Where did the kittens go on their class trip?
To a science mewseum.

....

**Chester: My parents got me a turtle for a pet
instead of a dog.**
Lester: Is having a pet turtle fun?
Chester: Not really. Watching him fetch a stick is kind of boring.

....

KOOKY QUESTION:
Do watchdogs get time off for good behavior?

....

What do you get when a pet pooch sees a ghost?
A dog fright.

....

Why was Mr. Doggie late for work?
He got tied up at home.

....

What do you do with a very sick dog?
Put him in an intensive cur unit.

....

What kind of parent does a mixed breed dog have?
A mutter.

....

Why did the boy give his dog a cell phone?
To make it easier to call him.

What did the owl say when he saw the kennel was empty?

Who let the dogs out?

Why was the old dog so happy?
He had a new leash on life.

Old Man: I'm taking our sick dog to the vet.
Old Lady: How can we afford to pay the bill?
Old Man: Don't worry. We have medicur.

Boy to Girl: My pet dog is a snazzy dresser. He wears a heavy coat in winter and pants in the summer.

How did the dog get splinters in his tongue?
He ate table scraps.

How do you make a dog dizzy?
Give it a tail spin.

What do you get if you cross a canine and a canary?
A doggie tweet.

Which dog weighs the most?
The heavyweight boxer.

Boy: Where is my pet pooch?
Mom: He ran away.
Boy: That's a doggone lie.

Ken: I took my dog to a pet psychologist, but it didn't do much good.
Len: Why not?
Ken: My dog is so well trained he refused to get on the couch.

How did Tom Cat learn he was a father?
His wife sent him a certified litter.

What does a pet pooch use to write a letter?
A dog pen.

Lady: My pet cat has a live bird in its mouth.
Vet: What kind of bird?
Lady: Swallow.
Vet: Don't say that!

What do you get if you cross a rabbit and two cats?
Hare! Kitty! Kitty!

Knock! Knock!
Who's there?
I Major.
I Major who?
I Major watchdog run away.

ATTENTION: Did you hear about the dog that went to medical school and became a famous heeler?

Uncle: How do you wake your son up in the morning?
Mother: I throw the neighbor's cat on his bed.
Uncle: How does that wake him up?
Mother: My son sleeps with his pet dog.

What did the dog say when he saw two tree trunks?
Bark! Bark!

Then there was the weary police dog who had a ruff day on the job.

What do you call a dog that is book smart?
A well-read Rover.

What do you call an old dog that can't see?
A blind spot.

What trick do you get when you cross a dog and an acrobat?
A bark flip.

What did Momma cat do after kitty soccer practice?
She picked up her litter.

Lana: I have a very cunning cat.
Donna: What makes you say that?
Lana: She eats a piece of cheese and then waits by a mouse hole with baited breath.

Mrs. Dog: Do you want to go to the flea market?
Mr. Dog: Yes. I'm itching to get there.

Pat: Look at all those happy dogs walking in single file.
Matt: That's the first time I ever saw a waggin' train.

What kind of dog tracks down new flowers?
A bud hound.

Farm Funnies

Why did the herd of sheep call the police?
They'd been fleeced by a con man.

. . . .

DAFFY DEFINITION: Shepherd: a sheep walker.

. . . .

Why did Mr. Duck get arrested?
The police caught him quacking a safe.

. . . .

What do you call a hen from Georgia who changes the color of her feathers?
Southern dyed chicken.

. . . .

What do you get if you cross an armored military vehicle with a sheep?
Tank ewe.

. . . .

What did the pig marshal say to the hog outlaw?
"Reach for the sty, pardner."

. . . .

What do you call a cow that always has bad luck?
A barn loser.

. . . .

What do you get if you cross a hog with a frog?
A hamphibian.

. . . .

What is a pig's favorite ballet?
Swine Lake.

Lester: Is Shakespeare the real name of your hog?

Chester: Nah. It's just his pen name.

....

Farmer: **Do you know how long cows should be milked?**

City Fella: **They should be milked the same as short cows are.**

....

What do you get if you cross a lemon grove and a herd of cows?

Lots of sour cream.

....

What do you get if you cross a cow with a tiger?

Something that's too dangerous to milk.

....

Knock! Knock!

Who's there?

Eject.

Eject who?

Eject the chicken coop and all the hens are gone.

....

Rooster: Would you like to give a speech to the hens?

Duck: I'll take a quack at it.

....

What do you do after you walk up to the front door of a bovine's home?

You ring the cow bell.

What's pigskin used for?

To hold the pig together.

....

Why did the rooster stick its head in the sand?

It was a beachcomber.

....

Then there was the exhausted shepherd who couldn't sheep at night.

....

Why did the pig get a bad grade in school?

He had sloppy penmanship.

....

What do you get if you put a dairy cow in a garden?

Milkweed.

....

Why was the farmhouse full of rabbits?

It had central hare conditioning.

....

What do you get if you cross a pig with a truck that says "wide load?"

A road hog.

....

Knock! Knock!

Who's there?

Mule.

Mule who?

Mule be sorry if you don't open the door.

What do you get if you cross a toad and a pig?

A wart hog.

. . . .

Why couldn't the good egg lend the poor rooster five bucks?

Because the egg was broke.

. . . .

Bunny Breeder: Some of my rabbit are kind of old.

Dairy Farmer: Having a few gray hares is nothing to be ashamed of.

. . . .

What do you get if you cross a holy relic with a bovine?

A sacred cow.

. . . .

Knock! Knock!
Who's there?
Hence.
Hence who?
Hence lay eggs in chicken coops.

. . . .

What did Barbie do when she directed the hens in a play?

Barbie cued the chickens.

. . . .

Poultry farmer: I bought fifty mail-order baby chickens and they haven't arrived yet.

Sales clerk: Relax. The chicks are in the mail.

When do baby hens leave their hotel?

At chickout time.

. . . .

Farmer: I own a skunk farm.

Reporter: Now that's a stinkin' way to earn a living.

. . . .

Farmer: Do you want to hear how I started my rabbit farm?

Reporter: No. I don't care for hare-raising tales.

Mr. Bull: I'm falling in love with you.

Ms. Cow: The feeling is mootual.

. . . .

Farmer: My donkey loves classical music.
Reporter: What's your donkey's name?
Farmer: Braytoven.

What sounds do you hear when you feed little chickens firecrackers?
Chick-a-boom! Chick-a-boom! Chick-a-boom! Boom! Boom!

Cow #1: Two bulls got into a savage fight yesterday.
Cow #2: Spare me the gory details.

Where does a hog leave its car when it takes the train to work?
In a pork and ride.

What do you get if you cross a pig and an angel?
Hog heaven.

Why do cows give milk?
They're not smart enough to sell it.

What do you call a sheep that squeals on her pals?
Ewe dirty rat.

What did Mr. Pig say to his girlfriend when he proposed marriage?
"Sty with me forever."

Mrs. Sheep: Anything interesting in tonight's newspaper?
Mr. Ram: No. It's all baa news.

Where do sheep get their hair cut?
At the local baa-baa shop.

Who was the strongest sheep in the ancient world?
Hercufleece.

Knock! Knock!
Who's there?
Ox.
Ox who?
Ox me nicely and I'll take you out for ice cream.

DAFFY DEFINITION:
Ram: A sheep that always butts in.

What do you call a sheep from outer space?
A Ewe-F-O.

Karate Pig: **How'd you like a pork chop?**
Boxer Sheep: **No thanks. How'd you like a wool sock?**
Tough Bunny: **Knock it off before I rabbit punch both of you.**

DAFFY DEFINITION:
Goat Herder: A person who likes to work with kids.

What did Captain Cattle say to Sergeant Steer?
Let's beef up our defenses.

What do you get if you cross a hog and a Texas lawman?
A pork ranger.

Then there was the dairy cow that started a lawn-mooing business.

What sound do you hear when you cross a cow with an owl?
Moo-who.

**What did the umpire yell when the pig
slid into home?**
"Pig out!"

PIG OUT!!

Tex: Was the All-Steer band any good?
Rex: Not really, but they had a good horn section.

> >

What do you get if you put a sheep in a steam room?
A wool sweater.

< < < < < < < < < < < < < < < < < < < < < < < <

Where do the Rockette Cow dancers perform?
Radio City Moosic Hall.

> >

Man: **What do you do for a living?**
Farmer: **I raise female pigs and male deer.**
Man: **Is that profitable?**
Farmer: **I already have one hundred sows and bucks.**

< < < < < < < < < < < < < < < < < < < < < < < <

What's the best way to keep milk fresh?
Leave it in the cow.

> > > > > > > > > > > > > >

NOTICE: **Dairy farmers want to make moo money.**

< < < < < < < < < < < < < <

What do Wall Street cows invest in?
Mootual funds.

> > > > > > > > > > > > >

Elsie: **Are you a newlywed cow?**
Dulcey: **Yes. I'm a honeymooer.**

< < < < < < < < < < < < <

What did the sailor say when he saw ewes swimming in the ocean?
Sheep ahoy!

> >

What does a rooster on a dairy farm shout at dawn?
Cock-a-doodle moo!

Why did the nanny goat quit her job?
She had too many kids to take care of.

◀ ◀ ◀ ◀ ◀ ◀ ◀ ◀ ◀ ◀ ◀ ◀ ◀ ◀ ◀ ◀ ◀ ◀ ◀

What do you call a goat that takes religious vows?
A nunny goat.

▶ ▶ ▶ ▶ ▶ ▶ ▶ ▶ ▶ ▶ ▶ ▶ ▶ ▶ ▶ ▶ ▶ ▶ ▶

When do cows make the most noise?
When they feel moo-dy.

◀ ◀ ◀ ◀ ◀ ◀ ◀ ◀ ◀ ◀ ◀ ◀ ◀ ◀ ◀ ◀ ◀ ◀ ◀

What did the bull say to his horns after they were trimmed?
"Having you around is pointless."

▶ ▶ ▶ ▶ ▶ ▶ ▶ ▶ ▶ ▶ ▶ ▶ ▶ ▶ ▶ ▶ ▶ ▶ ▶

What did the pasture say after the herd of cows left?
I'm not completely shot. They just grazed me.

◀ ◀ ◀ ◀ ◀ ◀ ◀ ◀ ◀ ◀ ◀ ◀ ◀ ◀ ◀ ◀ ◀ ◀ ◀

Knock! Knock!
Who's there?
Cow.
Cow who?
Cow much longer are you going to put up with all this knocking?

▶ ▶ ▶ ▶ ▶ ▶ ▶ ▶ ▶ ▶ ▶ ▶

What do you get if you cross a flock
of woolly animals and angels?
Sheep in heavenly peace.

◀ ◀ ◀ ◀ ◀ ◀ ◀ ◀ ◀ ◀ ◀ ◀

What has four wheels, two horns, and gives milk?
A cow on a skateboard.

▶ ▶ ▶ ▶ ▶ ▶ ▶ ▶ ▶ ▶ ▶ ▶

Shepherd #1: I heard wolves attack flocks at night.
Shepherd #2: So have I, but I'm not losing any sheep over it.

What has a woolly fleece and is combat ready?
A battle sheep.

Did you hear about the two shepherds who became best friends even though they had mutton in common?

Where do young cows eat their lunch?
In a calf-eteria.

What do you get if you cross a flock of sheep with a steer?
A woolly bully.

Why was Ms. Cow upset?
Her boyfriend was in a bullfight.

Why couldn't the dairy cow give milk?
She was an udder failure.

What's the easiest way to count your farm animals?
Use a cowculator.

Where do bovines go to enjoy fun in the sun?
Cowlifornia.

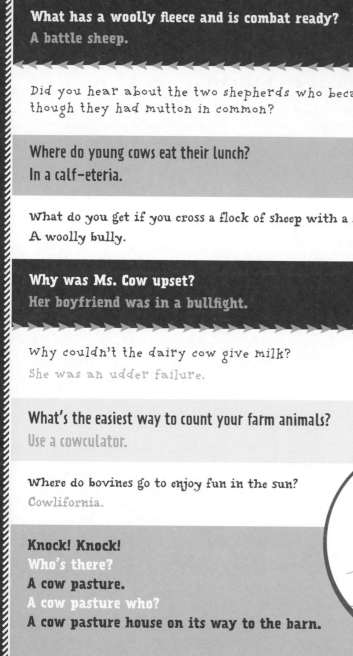

Knock! Knock!
Who's there?
A cow pasture.
A cow pasture who?
A cow pasture house on its way to the barn.

What do you get if when you leave dairy cows in the sun too long?
Evaporated milk.

What do you get if you cross a bovine and an ocean marker?
A cow buoy.

What do you get when a herd of dairy cows is caught in an earthquake?
Milkshakes.

Len: My uncle earns a living with his pen.
Ben: Is he a famous writer?
Len: No. He's a pig farmer.

What did Mr. Pig say to Ms. Hog?
"I wanna hold your ham."

What do you call a pig that robs houses?
A ham burglar.

Where does a ham burglar go if he gets caught?
To the state pen.

Knock! Knock!
Who's there?
Sty.
Sty who?
Sty home from school if you feel ill.

DAFFY DEFINITION:
Pig Farming: A real pork grind.

What kind of express train did the pig ride on? Ham track.

SIGN ON A PIG STY: Visitor porking only.

What do you call a slow hog? Pokey Pig.

Who was the most famous royal swine? Queen Pigtoria. ◄ ◄ ◄ ◄ ◄ ◄ ◄ ◄ ◄ ◄ ◄ ◄ ◄ ◄ ◄ ◄ ◄ ◄

What do you get when a pig eats an herb garden? Spiced ham.

What do you call a possessed pig? Deviled ham.

Knock! Knock! ◄ ◄ ◄ ◄ ◄ ◄ ◄ ◄ ◄ ◄ ◄ ◄ ◄ ◄ ◄ ◄ ◄ ◄ ◄
Who's there?
Pig.
Pig who?
Pig on someone your own size.

What do you get if you cross hogs and eagles? The day when pigs fly.

What does a pig eat after a big meal?
An after dinner oinkmint.

What do you call a pig that gets fired from its job?
A canned ham.

What does a pig eat on a hot day?
A slopsicle.

What did the hog say after it laid in the hot sun too long?
"I'm bacon out here."

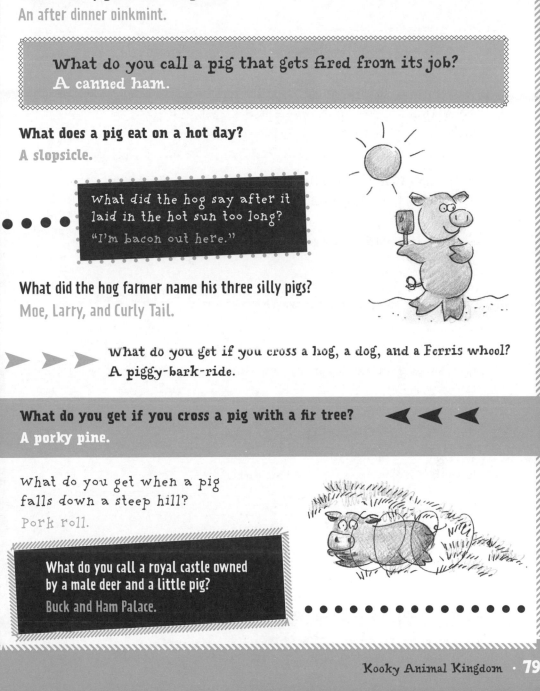

What did the hog farmer name his three silly pigs?
Moe, Larry, and Curly Tail.

What do you get if you cross a hog, a dog, and a Ferris wheel?
A piggy-bark-ride.

What do you get if you cross a pig with a fir tree?
A porky pine.

What do you get when a pig falls down a steep hill?
Pork roll.

What do you call a royal castle owned by a male deer and a little pig?
Buck and Ham Palace.

What does a pig bet in a game of cards?

Porker chips.

....

Mother Hen to her chicks at midnight: **"Now go to sleep and I don't want to hear another peep out of you."**

....

What farm animal comes in handy after a snowstorm?

The plow horse.

....

Zeke: **I know a hog that ate 100 dill cucumbers.**
Deke: **That's quite a pickled pig's feat.**

....

How do you safely handle a baby goat?

Use kid gloves.

....

Where does a pig go to pawn his watch?

At a ham hock shop.

....

Who has webbed feet and captures criminals?

Duck Tracy.

....

SIGN ON A CHICKEN COOP: **No fowl language!**

....

What do you get if you cross a pig with a gerbil?

A hamster.

....

Knock! Knock!
Who's there?
Aware, aware.
Aware, aware who?
Aware, aware have my little sheep gone?

What do you get if you cross a young sheep with a lumberjack?
Lamb chops.

What do you get if you cross a shelled nut with a ram?
A peanut butter.

SIGN ON A ROAD TO A SHEEP FARM: No ewe turns.

What did the sheep say to the ram?
Hey, move your butt!

What hen was the first chicken in space?
Cluck Rogers.

Sheep: I'm going to tell you about the most powerful sheep in history.
Goat: Oh no. Not more bleats of strength.

Why did the two flocks of sheep have an accident?
They rammed into each other.

Why was the rooster upset?
He couldn't find his comb.

NOTICES:
Acme Wool, Inc.: **We're a tightly-knit company.**
Acme Wool Products: **We're the best and it's the darn truth.**

The little pig who lived in a house of bricks: We made the Big Bad Wolf so mad he left in a huff!

NOTICE: All cattle in the American West have a brand name.

Why did Mr. Pig go to the casino?
He wanted to play the slop machines.

What do you find at a hog mall?
Pork shops.

What do you call a chicken that eats hard clay?
A brick layer.

What do you get when a sow has a cranky baby pig?
The ham that rocks the cradle.

NOTICES:
Computer sheep use ewe tube.
Cows have Hay-T-M cards.
Crows have cawling cards.
Cavalry horses have charge cards.

What did Captain Pig shout to his crew?
All hams on deck.

What kind of bird insults people?

A mocking bird.

....

What does a bison bet in Las Vegas?

Buffalo chips.

....

How does a poultry farmer keep track of newborn chickens?

He makes notes in his chick book.

....

Knock! Knock!
Who's there?
Ewe.
Ewe who?
Ewe look familiar to me.

....

What happens when you talk to a cow?

It goes in one ear and out the udder.

....

CHAPTER 2

SCHOOL SNICKERS

What class did the demolition crew take?
Home wreckonomics.

. . . .

What do you get if you cross a teacher and a golf coach?
Book clubs.

. . . .

What comes at the end of a jail sentence?
A free period.

. . . .

Why did the clock get detention?
It kept tocking in class.

. . . .

What school activity does Jack Frost like best?
Snow and Tell.

. . . .

Teacher: **Did your father help you with these math problems?**
Student: **No, teacher. I got them wrong all by myself.**

. . . .

Knock! Knock!
Who's there?
Ivan.
Ivan who?
Ivan sent to the office three times today.

. . . .

Basketball Coach: Today I'm giving you a test on how to make assists.
Player: What do we have to do?
Basketball Coach: Just pass and you'll pass.

. . . .

Why didn't the biology teacher marry the physics teacher?
The chemistry just wasn't right.

Jenny: I'm reading a sob story.

Penny: Can I borrow it when you're finished?

Jenny: Yes. You're welcome to read it and weep.

....

Why didn't the French teacher ask the Spanish teacher to marry him?

He didn't know how to speak the language of love.

....

How do bee students get to class?
They take a school buzz.

....

What's the difference between a locomotive engineer and a school teacher?

One minds the train and the other trains the mind.

....

Why did the rabbit try out for high school sports?

He wanted to go to the Varsity Hop.

....

Why did the comedian tell school jokes?

He wanted to have a class act.

....

Teacher: Our president is married to the First Lady.

Girl: I thought Adam was married to the first lady.

Knock! Knock!

Who's there?

Alda.

Alda who?

Alda kids in my class are taller than me.

....

Boy: Do hens get marks for laying eggs?

Girl: No, but they grade the eggs.

What do you get if you cross a math teacher and a clock?

Arithmaticks.

....

What English college did the bull go to?
Oxford.

....

What did the teacher say to the rabbit student?

Sit hare.

....

Why do elephant students always get good grades?

Because elephants never forget to study.

How does a gym teacher keep evil spirits out of the gym?

He exorcises them.

....

Gym Teacher: What is your favorite aquatic sport?

Student: Channel surfing.

....

What's the first class a snake takes in school?

Hisstory.

....

What do pig students bring home at the end of a semester?

Repork cards.

Why does it take snails six years to graduate from high school?

Snails are slow learners.

Why was the student Jolly Green Giant so sad?

He didn't do well on his pea SATs.

....

Zack: Why did you go to boarding school?

Mack: Dude! I thought it was a surfer's college.

....

Music Teacher: Why did you sign up for violin lessons?

Student: I just wanted to fiddle around.

....

Why did the sailor play high school sports?

Because he wanted to be elected captain.

....

Knock! Knock!
Who's there?
Weevil.
Weevil who?
Weevil heard enough about the Civil War for one day.

....

Cara: Basket-making class is cancelled.

Lara: Why?

Cara: The teacher took a weave of absence.

NOTICE: Troll Students are gnome schooled.

What comes out at night and hoots, "Whom? What? Where?"
A wise owl showing off his vocabulary.

Why did the baby genius take geometry?
He wanted to learn about formulas.

Why did the farmer take a math class?
He wanted to learn about square roots.

Student: Do you have any books on card games?
Librarian: You bet we do.

Jack: I read a book on how they made the Holland and Lincoln tunnels.
Mack: Boring!

In a Catholic school the librarian is a Sister. She's also an expert on nun-fiction.

Boy: **Can you help me pick out some good books to read?**
Librarian: **I'm sorry, but this is a shelf-service library.**

What flies around a kindergarten class at night?
The alphabat.

Which fish is always last?
The one in the after-school program.

Which cartoon skunk is a college bound student?
Preppy Le Phew!

Where did the smart cat go to college?
Purr-due.

What is Mickey's job at school?
He's the mice principal.

Mom: How did you manage to get an A in art class?
Daughter: I was picture perfect.

Why didn't 2 go out with 3?
He was a little odd.

Boy: **Summer vacation is getting to be too short.**
Girl: **What do you mean?**
Boy: **It's not long enough for me to forget what I learned in school all year.**

Girl: I want to take my college classes on a cruise ship.
Advisor: First you have to go to boarding school.

Father: **Did your chemistry teacher like your class project?**
Boy: **He loved it. In fact, it blew him away.**

Why are fish great at doing math?
They multiply fast.

Teacher: **What was Samuel Clemens' pen name?**
Student: **Convict?**

Boy: My teacher talks to herself.
Father: Does she know that?
Boy: Nah. She thinks we're listening to her.

Teacher: Today we're having an I.Q. test.
Dork: Oh no! I forgot to study for it.

►►►►►►►►►►►►►►►►►►►►

What did the astronaut give the school bully?

His launch money.

◄◄◄◄◄◄◄◄◄◄◄◄◄◄◄◄◄◄◄

What do you do with a naughty principal?
Make him sit in a corner office.

►►►►►►►►►►►►►►►►►►►►

Why did the banker become a teacher?

She wanted to check papers.

◄◄◄◄◄◄◄◄◄◄◄◄◄◄◄◄◄◄◄

Johnny: I want to study sources of energy in college.
Lonnie: Maybe you'll win a fuel scholarship.

►►►►►►►►►►►►►►►►►►►►

Knock! Knock!
Who's there?
Will Hugh.
Will Hugh who?
Will Hugh all pass in last night's homework, please?

◄◄◄◄◄◄◄◄◄◄◄◄◄◄◄◄◄◄◄

Why wouldn't numbers 9 and 3 play ball against numbers 5 and 7?
Because the teams weren't even.

►►►►►►►►►►►►►►►►►►►►

Then there was the absent-minded conductor who
frequently lost his train of thought.

◄◄◄◄◄◄◄◄◄◄◄◄◄◄◄◄◄◄◄

How do you paint a research facility?
First put on a lab coat.

SIGN IN GYM: Watch your step. No class trips.

◄ ◄

Knock! Knock!
Who's there?
Water.
Water who?
Water you waiting for? Get to class.

► ►

Father: **Does my son fool around in school?**
Principal: **Let me put it this way. He has a reserved seat outside my office.**

◄ ◄

Teacher: Today we're going to watch a history lesson on TV and I don't want anyone changing the subject.

► ►

NOTICE: Student umpires who want to learn how to call balls and strikes are home-schooled.

◄ ◄

Why did the architect become a school teacher?
He wanted to draw up some lesson plans.

► ►

Why did the teacher bring birdseed to school?
She had a parrot-teacher conference after class.

◄ ◄ ◄ ◄ ◄ ◄ ◄ ◄ ◄ ◄ ◄ ◄

Where did the plum go to college?
U. of Pitt.

► ► ► ► ► ► ► ► ► ►

Knock! Knock!
Who's there?
Sum.
Sum who?
Sum math teachers are harder than others.

What did the bully say to his instructor?
Go ahead. I dare you to teach me a lesson.

What does the person in charge of a school eat a noontime?
The principal meal of the day.

How much schooling did the famous detective Sherlock Holmes have?
Just elementary stuff.

Teacher: How did you like our lesson about the Atlantic Ocean?
Student: I couldn't absorb all of the information.

What do you call a TV set outside of class?
A hall monitor.

Girl: **What are you reading?**
Boy: **A mystery.**
Girl: **But that's a math textbook.**
Boy: **It's a mystery to me.**

Grandfather: **How could you do so badly in history? I always excelled in this class.**
Grandson: **That's because there was less history to study when you were in school.**

Teacher: What grade are you in, soldier?
Military School Student: Sixth, sir. But I'm expecting a promotion at the end of the year.

SIGN IN ART CLASS: Fingerpaints ... a hands-on activity.

What do you get if you cross a rat with a best-selling author?
A rodent with a lot of tales.

Student Chef: I took a course on how to prepare tender steak. It was a tough class to pass.

NOTICE TO COMMERCIAL FISHERMEN: No school today.

Harry: I want to go to lumber school.
Barry: First you have to pass your college boards.

Why did the student with the flu have to stay after school?
His nose kept running in the halls.

What was the name of the Quiz Kid's father?
Pop Quiz.

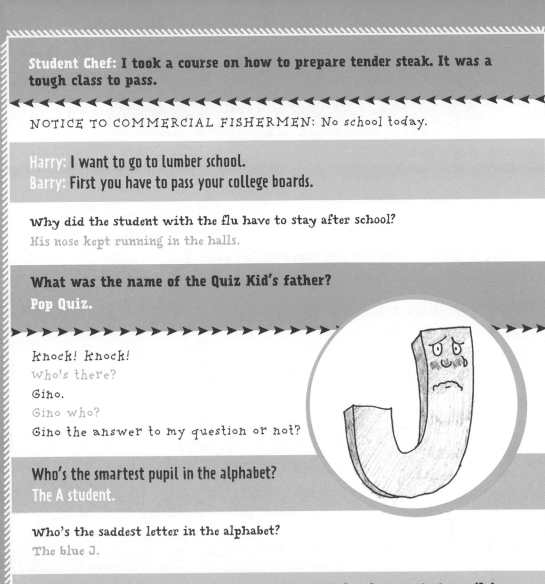

Knock! Knock!
Who's there?
Gino.
Gino who?
Gino the answer to my question or not?

Who's the smartest pupil in the alphabet?
The A student.

Who's the saddest letter in the alphabet?
The blue J.

Which two letters of the alphabet announce who the smartest pupil in your class is?
I–M.

Why was the math teacher upset?
His son was a problem child.

What did the junior high basketball team do at snack time?
They dunked doughnuts.

Jack: My teacher always picks on me and makes fun of me.
Mack: So transfer to another class.
Jack: I can't. I'm home-schooled.

Why was Miss Smith's class a total circus?
Too many of her students were class clowns.

Where do convicts go to college?
Penn State.

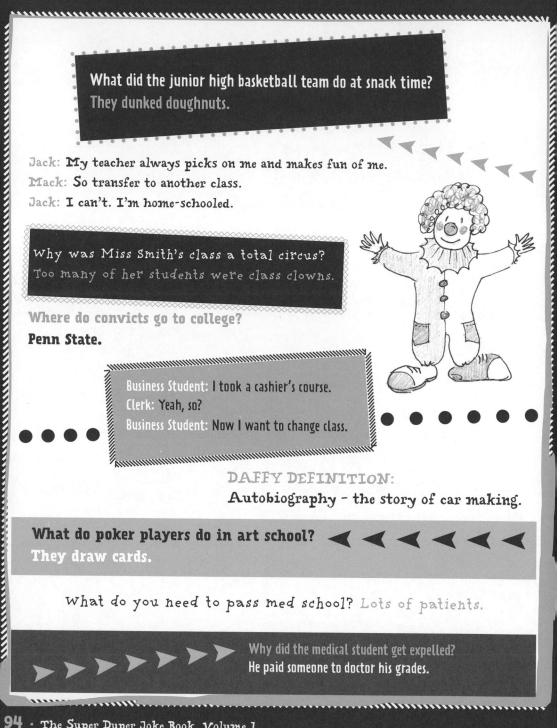

Business Student: I took a cashier's course.
Clerk: Yeah, so?
Business Student: Now I want to change class.

DAFFY DEFINITION:
Autobiography - the story of car making.

What do poker players do in art school?
They draw cards.

What do you need to pass med school? Lots of patients.

Why did the medical student get expelled?
He paid someone to doctor his grades.

What is the worst bug you can find in a medical school dorm?
The flu bug.

Lily: What are you going to do in the school talent show?
Billy: I'm going to pretend to be a bird flying.
Lily: In other words, you're going to act up.

Knock! Knock!
Who's there?
Adopt.
Adopt who?
Adopt my pen on the floor and it rolled away.

Bill: Did you climb the ropes in gym?
Will: Yes. For a few minutes I was at the top of my class.

Student: What grade did I get on The Old Man and the Sea?
Teacher: You're the Young Man and the C.

Latin Student: Are you good in Spanish class?
Spanish Student: Si!
Latin Student: Oh well, we can't all be "A" students.

Gym Teacher: Tomorrow we're going to jump rope.
Girl: Yahoo! I finally get to skip class.

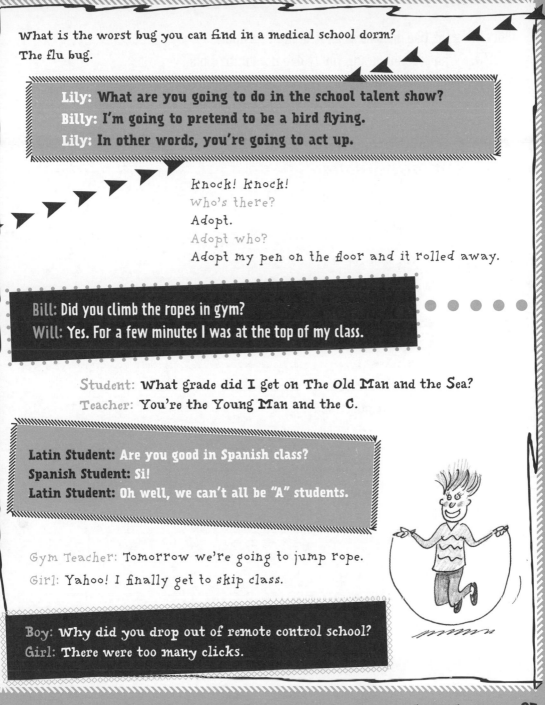

Boy: Why did you drop out of remote control school?
Girl: There were too many clicks.

Boy: I'm a lot like my dad when it comes to school.

Teacher: What do you mean? You're dad is a businessman.

Boy: I know, but we both always need extra credit to get by.

....

DAFFY DEFINITION:

Addition Problem — sum fun.

....

What do you get if you cross teachers and lawyers?

A class-action suit.

....

What class does Mr. Soda Pop teach?

Fizz Ed.

....

DAFFY DEFINITION:

Drama School Play – a class act.

....

Why did the police detective go to school?

To investigate the student body.

....

Coach: Will you please pass the mustard?

Teacher: I show no favoritism at grading time.

....

How does an acrobat read a school book?

He flips through the pages.

....

What does teacher Santa mail to homes?

Christmas report cards.

....

Why did the geek take his report to the school dance?

The teacher told him to date his paper.

Why are teachers like bank robbers?
They both want everyone to raise
their hands.

$2 + 2 =$ ___
$3 + 2 =$ ___

Then there was the math teacher who
wore plus-size clothes.

What is a kangaroo student's favorite part
of the year?
Spring break.

What's yellow, has wheels, and attends classes?
Student buses.

Why did the dentist go back to medical school?
He wanted to brush up on his studies.

What did the fish give his teacher?
A crabapple.

Jenny: Why did you drop out of medical school?
Lenny: I'm sick of doing homework.

Why did the surgeon become a watchmaker?
He wanted to be a big-time operator.

What does it take to pass a course on intestines?
A lot of guts.

KOOKY QUESTION:
Does a gymnastics coach take roll call?

And then there was the history teacher who insisted on living in the past.

DAFFY DEFINITION:
Female Astronaut — a launch lady.

Ted: I got an "A" for cutting class.
Fred: What? How's that possible?
Ted: I go to barber school.

What do you use to catch a school of fish?
Bookworms.

What does a real-estate student do after school?
He has lots to study.

Where do rabbits go to medical school?
They go to Johns Hop-kins.

Robbie: Someday I want to help build the perfect fighting man.
Bobbie: Study marine biology.

Knock! Knock!
Who's there?
Anita.
Anita who?
Anita borrow a pencil and some paper.

Why did the caddy go back to school?
He wanted to study golf courses.

What do band students sit on?
Musical chairs.

Why couldn't the student flyer become a test pilot?
His grades weren't high enough.

What is a home-schooled student's first class?
Home room.

Why is a school like a kingdom?
They both have many subjects.

NOTICE: I don't mind being sent to the office so much ... it's the principal of the thing that really bugs me.

What do you get if you cross a sorcerer with a class instructor?
A wiz ed teacher.

DAFFY DEFINITION:

School Library — a silence museum.

Why was the cat student given an award at the end of the year?

It had a purrfect attendance record.

Why is a schoolyard larger at recess than at any other time?

Because at recess there are more feet in it.

. . . .

Why did an alarm sound when a monk walked into school?

It was time for a friar drill.

. . . .

Student: **What do I have to do to graduate from this music school?**

Teacher: **Just pass notes.**

. . . .

Why did the girl get a bad grade in cooking class?

Her dog ate her homework.

How To Tell a Joke!

Making people laugh isn't as easy as it looks—though messing up a joke is incredibly easy! Comedians practice telling their jokes over and over until they have them just right. Follow these tips and your audience will be giggling and guffawing!

1. Know your joke by heart. Practice it out loud before telling it to your audience. And then tell it with confidence.

2. The lead up to a joke is important. Don't tell your audience you're about to tell the joke. Just tell it. Surprise is a big part of the humor. Also, don't tell them ahead of time how funny (or dumb or not funny) your joke is. (There's nothing funny about that).

3. Practice timing your punch line. It's called punch line for a reason!

4. Provide just enough details so that the joke works. Don't overdo it.

5. Don't tell jokes you don't get.

6. Watch the pros tell jokes and mimic their styles while you develop your own style.

TEACHER SEZ ...

Today we're going to study about growing a garden. Take out your weeding books.

Today we're going to study pigs. Does everyone have a pen?

Today I'm going to put a new spin on computer learning. Take out your lap tops.

Today we're going to talk about death. And this will be on your final exam.

How does a clam open its hall locker?

It uses a seafood combination.

Boy: **Two of my classes at school are brothers.**

Father: **Which two?**

Boy: **Jim Class and Art Class.**

What did the teacher say to the pirate during the test?

Keep your ayes on your own paper.

Why did the bulldozer operator become a teacher?

He wanted to grade exams.

Knock! Knock!

Who's there?

Ozzie.

Ozzie who?

Ozzie absent from class today?

What's the best way to pass a chef's exam?

Cook up some great answers.

What do you call a teacher's assistant who's from another country?
Foreign aide.

What do you call a part-time music instructor who gives trumpet lessons?

A substi-toot teacher.

Teacher: What do you like best about bakery school?
Student: Roll call.

Why was the student sheep so sad?
She flunked her baaology test.

Why did the carpenter sign up for math class?

He wanted to study up on home additions.

What do three classroom feet equal?
A school yard.

Boy: Dad, I think I'm in a school for snails.
Dad: What makes you say that?
Boy: On the road that leads to the building there's a sign that reads, "Slow School Ahead."

Hal: We're all going to join the school math club.
Cal: Well, count me out.

What did the computer say when the student asked it a homework question?
Search me!

▶ ▶

ATTENTION: No tennis classes — In-service day.

◀ ◀

Why did the military school student guard his textbooks?
His teachers told him to cover his books.

▶ ▶

Why did Romeo and Juliet study Spanish and French?
Because Spanish and French are romance languages.

◀ ◀

Teacher: **Start counting at five and keep going.**

Student: **Five, six, seven, eight, nine, ten, jack, queen, king, ace.**

Teacher: **Whoa! You've been watching too many poker shows on TV.**

▶ ▶

Knock! Knock!
Who's there?
Weird.
Weird who?
Weird you get the answers to this test?

◀ ◀

What kind of book should you bring to music class?
A note pad.

▶ ▶

What did the math student say to the algebra problem?
I just can't figure you out.

What did the math student say to the geometry teacher?
You know all the angles!

◄ ◄ ◄ ◄ ◄ ◄ ◄ ◄ ◄ ◄ ◄ ◄

Why did the young teacher take diving lessons?
He wanted to work as a sub.

► ► ► ► ► ► ► ► ► ► ► ►

NOTICE: Then there were the two music students who fell in love and sent romantic notes to each other.

◄ ◄ ◄ ◄ ◄ ◄ ◄ ◄ ◄ ◄ ◄

ASSIGNMENT IN A COOKING CLASS: Do your home wok.

► ► ► ► ► ► ► ► ► ► ► ► ► ► ► ►

Boy: My teacher doesn't know the difference between math and grammar.
Father: What do you mean?
Boy: She keeps talking about add-verbs.

◄ ◄ ◄ ◄ ◄ ◄ ◄ ◄ ◄ ◄ ◄ ◄ ◄

Teacher: Is Morgan Matthews here?
Melanie: Morgan is absent, teacher.
Teacher: Quiet, Melanie. Let Morgan speak for himself.

► ► ► ► ► ► ► ► ► ► ► ► ► ► ► ► ►

What has four wheels and discovered America?
Christopher Colum-bus.

◄ ◄ ◄ ◄ ◄ ◄ ◄ ◄ ◄ ◄ ◄ ◄ ◄

What did the student give his music teacher?
A note from home.

► ► ► ► ► ► ► ► ► ► ► ► ► ► ► ►

Teacher: In order for their species to survive, animals must breed.
Student: Duh! If animals didn't breed, they'd suffocate.

SOME SILLY TEACHERS:
Mr. Mark R. Exams
Ms. Kim S. Tree
Mr. M. T. Halls
Mr. Tex Booker
Mr. Hugh Flunk

Why did the zombie student take Latin Class?
Because Latin is a dead language.

Why was the astronaut late for school?
He forgot his launchbox and had to go back for it.

Teacher: How do you think you did on the test?
Student: You'll be surprised. Mark my words.

What kind of essay does a tough judge write?
One that has lots of long sentences.

What has feathers and gives yearly physicals?
The school ducktor.

What do you get if you cross an addition
problem with a rabbit's foot?
Sum luck.

What do you get if you cross an art teacher with a math teacher?
A color-by-numbers project.

What happened to Miss Cherry?
She graduated at the top of her sundae school class.

Teacher: What are the three words I never want to hear spoken in my class?
Student: I don't know.
Teacher: That's correct.

What color should a good book be?
A good book should be well red.

Knock! Knock!
Who's there?
Chauffeur.
Chauffeur who?
Chauffeur this semester I've received two As and a B.

What goes caw, caw, caw and does jumping jacks?
A crow-ed gym class.

Knock! Knock!
Who's there?
Luke.
Luke who?
Luke over all the notes I gave you.

What do you get if you cross an exam with a trunk?
A test case.

Millie: I went to school to learn how to shop better.
Tillie: What did you study?
Millie: Buyology.

Willie: I'm going to clown college.
Nilly: Did you get a fool scholarship?

What do you get if you cross a sheep with a clown?

Ewe make me laugh.

What did the school nurse say to the sick students at Clown College?

Remember, laughter is the best medicine.

Brad: I met my girlfriend at Clown College.

Chad: How was the romance?

Brad: It's a funny story.

Judy: How did you manage to graduate from Clown College?

Rudy: The teachers always laughed at my exam answers.

Why did a duck play the bass drum on the school band?

He was an expert on the down beat.

What do you get if you cross a clown college with a school for accountants?

Funny business.

How do you find a clown college on the Internet?
Google Giggles.

Knock! Knock!
Who's there?
Chuckle.
Chuckle who?
Chuckle make you laugh, won't you Chuck?

Professor: When I give a test at Clown College, I expect a lot of funny business during the exam.

What do you get if you cross a clown with Big Foot?
Laugh tracks.

Benny: How did you guys pass your test at Clown College?
Lenny: We crammed together for the clown car exam.

Knock! Knock!
Who's there?
I Rhoda.
I Rhoda who?
I Rhoda book and I hope it becomes a bestseller.

Larry: I wrote a book about rating basements.
Barry: What's it called?
Larry: The Best Cellar List.

Jim: I wrote a book about the Prince of England.
Tim: Did the publisher offer you a good deal?
Jim: Yes. I got a royalty contract.

. . . .

Mick: I knew an author who wrote a funny book about wood carving.
Rick: What kind of book is that?
Mick: A joke and whittle book.

. . . .

FUNNY FORGETTABLE TITLES:

BATHROOM HUMOR by Hugo Potty
OLD FURNITURE by Anne Teek
EASY DANCE LESSONS by B.N. Stepp
LIVING ALONE by Buzz Hoff
DIRTY JOKES by Anita Bath

. . . .

What did the drum say to the drumstick?
You think you're so tough just because you can beat me.

. . . .

What do you get if you cross a school band
and football spikes?

A halftime shoe.

. . . .

Where does a cat band march?
In purr-ades.

. . . .

What did the infielder play in the school band.
A base fiddle.

. . . .

**What should you give a drum majorette
who skins her knee?**
A Band-aid.

What did Teacher Clock say to the student clocks?
Keep your hands to yourselves.

. . . .

Mr. Bird: **What are you studying in school?**
Little Bird: **Owl-gebra.**

. . . .

What do you get if you cross band members
and sports fans?
Musical cheers.

. . . .

Bessie: **What do the students do at Clown College?**
Tessie: **We just fool around.**

. . . .

NOTICE: Clown College is the place where every student is a class clown.

. . . .

Why did the cat go to Clown College?
It wanted to be a giggle puss.

. . . .

Why did the hare go to Clown College?
It wanted to be a funny bunny.

. . . .

Why is Clown College a pleasure to attend?
The classes are like a three-ring circus.

. . . .

Why did the student take an anatomy class at Clown College?
He wanted to learn how to tickle the funny bone.

. . . .

Knock! Knock!
Who's there?
Grin.
Grin who?
Grin you're smiling, the whole world smiles with you.

What animal is the mascot of the Clown College?

A laughing hyena.

. . . .

Teacher: How did you like the story of Dr. Jekyll and Mr. Hyde?
Student: It was good and bad.

. . . .

Art Teacher: This work of art depicts fall sports.
Student: What's it called?
Art Teacher: Collage football.

. . . .

How do you get to be a cosmetologist?
Take a makeup test.

. . . .

What did the dork study in college?
Geek mythology.

. . . .

What pirate skipped school a lot?
Captain Hookey.

. . . .

What do you get if you cross a sardine with a math teacher?
A herring problem.

. . . .

Barry: **That parrot is talking about American history, math problems, and English literature.**
Larry: **That's because it used to be a teacher's pet.**

Why didn't the little nose like going to school?
Because everyone there picked on him.

. . . .

Why did the mime student get detention?
He talked in class.

. . . .

What did Buffalo Bill say when his boy left for college?
Bison.

How did the Hobbit learn to read?
He studied the elfabet.

. . . .

What are the instructions for a mime test?
Words fail me.

. . . .

Uncle: **I heard you studied art and logic at college.**
Nephew: **Yes. Now I'm able to draw my own conclusions.**

How do you become an A-plus carpenter?

Do a lot of homework.

....

NOTICE: Bilbo Baggins was gnome schooled.

....

Teacher: Have you read any Dr. Seuss books?

Boy: Hey! I'm a middle school student, not a medical school student.

....

Why couldn't the pig get a student loan?

His parents had a bad credit repork.

....

Teacher: George Washington went down in history.

Student: So did I. I dropped from a B to a C plus.

....

Mother: **How do you like learning addition in school?**

Son: **Every day it's the sum old story.**

....

What do you get if you cross a music teacher with a mechanic?

Someone who knows how to tune up a car engine.

....

Teacher: What did Caesar say when Brutus stabbed him?

Boy: Ouch!

Knock! Knock!
Who's there?
Ken Hugh.
Ken Hugh who?
Ken Hugh help me with my book report?

....

ATTENTION: Old school principals never become senile ... they just lose their faculties.

....

Teacher: **Why are you late for gym class?**
Student: **I sprained my ankle in the hall.**
Teacher: **That's a lame excuse.**

....

Teacher: **Why is your report on milk so short?**

Boy: **I wrote it on condensed milk.**

Boy: **I added up these same numbers ten times.**

Teacher: **That's the way to check your work. Now what did you get?**

Boy: **Ten different answers.**

KOOKY QUESTION: If teachers are so smart, why do they spend the school day asking so many questions?

Preschool Teacher: Where does milk come from?
Little Girl: The dairy case.

Teacher: What are taxes?
Boy: Small nails.

Teacher: The law of gravity keeps us from falling off the earth.
Girl: What kept us from falling off before the law was passed?

Boy: My teacher can't read my handwriting.
Father: That's bad. Write more clearly from now on.
Boy: No, it's good. If I write more clearly she'll find out I can't spell.

Boy: Did you say ice cream?
Teacher: No. You always speak softly.

Gary: Did you hear the news? My algebra teacher just divorced your calculus teacher.
Mary: Humph! Go figure.

What kind of soup does a student studying for exams eat?
Cram chowder.

Teacher: How much is eight minus eight?
Student: I have nothing to say.

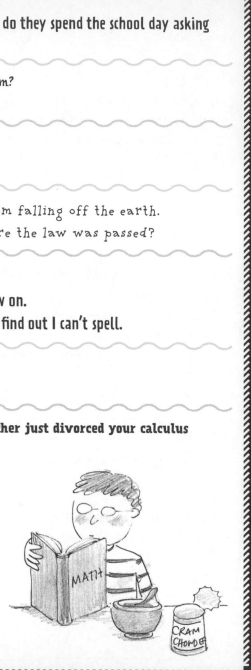

Denny: This new math looks fishy to me.

Lenny: Maybe they're herring problems.

Lilly: I heard that the algebra teacher likes the geometry teacher, but she likes the calculus teacher.

Millie: Gosh! What a wacky love triangle.

What did the algebra teacher say to the morning mist?

Dew the math.

Girl: I'm so good at jump rope class my gym teacher let me skip a year.

Teacher: What's topsoil?

Boy: A dirty word.

Teacher: What does it mean when the barometer falls?

Boy: It means the person who put it up did a lousy job.

Algebra Teacher: And so in conclusion we find that X is equal to zero.

Student: Oh brother! All that work for nothing.

What do you get if you cross a teacher and a lawyer?

A test case.

Teacher: Do you take the school bus home?

Boy: I'd like to, but it won't fit in our garage.

Music Teacher: Can you play the trumpet?

Boy: You're darn tooting I can!

History Teacher: When Abe Lincoln lived in Washington he had a goatee.

Boy: Gosh. Wasn't that a strange pet to keep in the White House?

▶ ▶ ▶ ▶ ▶ ▶ ▶ ▶ ▶ ▶ ▶ ▶ ▶ ▶ ▶ ▶ ▶ ▶ ▶ ▶

Professor: Today I'll lecture on the heart, liver, kidneys, and lungs.

Medical Student: Oh no! Not another organ recital.

◀ ◀ ◀ ◀ ◀ ◀ ◀ ◀ ◀ ◀ ◀ ◀ ◀ ◀ ◀ ◀ ◀ ◀ ◀ ◀

Marty: I have a sister and two brothers.

Teacher: Are you the oldest in the family?

Marty: No way. My mom and dad are older than I am.

▶ ▶ ▶ ▶ ▶ ▶ ▶ ▶ ▶ ▶ ▶ ▶ ▶ ▶ ▶ ▶ ▶ ▶ ▶ ▶

Mindy: How did you do on your pastry chef exam?

Cindy: I passed with flying crullers.

◀ ◀ ◀ ◀ ◀ ◀ ◀ ◀ ◀ ◀ ◀ ◀ ◀ ◀ ◀ ◀ ◀ ◀ ◀ ◀

SIGN IN A SCHOOL FOR STUDENT MIMES: Absolutely no talking.

▶ ▶ ▶ ▶ ▶ ▶ ▶ ▶ ▶ ▶ ▶ ▶ ▶ ▶ ▶ ▶ ▶ ▶ ▶ ▶

Teacher: Jamie your drawing of a stagecoach is very good, but it has no wheels. What holds it up?

Jamie: Outlaws.

◀ ◀ ◀ ◀ ◀ ◀ ◀ ◀ ◀ ◀

Teacher: Why don't many people live in Alaska?

Student: Because it's snow far away.

▶ ▶ ▶ ▶ ▶ ▶ ▶ ▶ ▶ ▶

Teacher: Are all classrooms getting new blackboards before school opens?

Principal: Yes. We want every student to start the year with a clean slate.

Teacher: Did you read the book about trees I gave you?

Student: I leafed through it.

◄ ◄ ◄ ◄ ◄ ◄ ◄ ◄ ◄ ◄ ◄ ◄ ◄ ◄ ◄ ◄ ◄

Sam and Pam walked into a deli. They were both philosophy students at a nearby college. When a waiter came over, Sam ordered a chicken sandwich and an egg salad sandwich for himself. After the waiter left, Pam asked Sam. "Why did you do that?" Sam grinned. "It's an experiment," said he. "I wanted to see which comes first, the chicken or the egg."

► ► ► ► ► ► ► ► ► ► ► ► ► ► ► ► ►

Fred: My health teacher said that exercise will kill germs.

Ed: I guess he knows what's he's talking about.

Fred: But how do you get germs to exercise?

◄ ◄ ◄ ◄ ◄ ◄ ◄ ◄ ◄ ◄ ◄ ◄ ◄ ◄ ◄ ◄ ◄

Student: When rain falls, does it eventually go back up into the sky?

Teacher: Yes. In dew time.

► ► ► ► ► ► ► ► ► ► ► ► ► ► ► ► ►

Why do math teachers make good detectives?

They're great at putting two and two together.

◄ ◄ ◄ ◄ ◄ ◄ ◄ ◄ ◄ ◄ ◄ ◄ ◄ ◄ ◄ ◄ ◄

A teacher asked her third grade students to write down what each one thought was the greatest mystery of nature. Barney Barns wrote that he thought a bear's coat was the greatest mystery of nature. "Why do you think a bear's coat is the greatest mystery of nature Barney?" asked the teacher. Replied the student, "Because God only knows where it's buttoned."

► ► ► ► ► ► ► ► ► ► ► ► ► ► ► ► ►

Who do you get if you cross a phys. Ed teacher and a famous western scout?

Gym Bridger.

◄ ◄ ◄ ◄ ◄ ◄ ◄ ◄ ◄ ◄ ◄ ◄ ◄ ◄ ◄ ◄ ◄

Teacher: Do you know the name of this Scandinavian country?

Surfer: Nor way, dude.

Teacher: Are you going to finish your woodcarving project for art class?
Student: No. And let the chips fall where they may.

What kind of theology students wear ice skates?
Hockey prayers.

A college theology student was given an exam on biblical holidays. He was stumped by an essay question so he wrote; "Only God knows the answer to this question." Three days later he got back his exam. Next to his essay question his professor wrote, "God gets an A, but you get an F."

Principal: **Why are your students buzzing?**
Teacher: **They're getting ready for a spelling bee.**

Teacher: Can you name the four seasons?
Boy: Pepper, salt, vinegar, and mustard.

Why was the inchworm angry?
His teacher was making him convert to the metric system.

Why didn't the math teacher buy a farm?
He thought some problems might crop up.

What happened to the geometry teacher who became a sailor?
She got lost in the Bermuda Triangle.

"Class I want you to use the word 'bean' in a sentence," said the teacher.

"My father raised a bean crop," said the farmer's son.

"My mother made a three-bean casserole last night," said the chef's daughter.

"You're all bean brains," said the boy whose father was a comedian.

A pessimist is a student who puts a zero on his exam when his teacher hands him the test.

Why did the teacher let the firefly leave the classroom?

Because when you've got to glow you've got to glow.

A little boy came home from his first day at a new school. "How do you like your teacher?" his mother asked him. "I don't like her," the boy quickly replied. "But why not?" questioned the mom. "Because she told me to sit up front for the present," he huffed, "and then she never gave me the gift."

Lunchtime Laughs

Why wasn't the astronaut's son in the cafeteria?
He went home for launch.

Where does Jack Frost sit in the cafeteria?
With the cool kids.

Teacher #1: I usually skip lunch and jog instead.
Teacher #2: I jog at lunchtime, too, but I eat on the run.

When does a sandwich ask a lot of questions?
When it's made with why bread.

NOTICE: The food at the medical school cafeteria is so bad that with every meal you get a free prescription!

Where do math teachers go for their noonday meal?
To a lunch counter.

Teacher: If you had six potatoes to divide between twelve people. What would you do?
Student: Mash the potatoes.

Principal: Why are you late for school?
Student: I'm not late for school, I'm early for lunch.

What do you get if a ghost flies into the school cafeteria?
A food fright.

What do members of the school baseball team eat their lunches on?
Home plates.

What did the clumsy student say after he spilled his soup?
Don't worry everyone, lunch is on me.

What does a horn player use to brush his teeth?
A tuba toothpaste.

SIGN IN A SCHOOL LUNCHROOM: Ask for our senior discount.

Teacher: **I'd like to know what's in the stew you're serving for lunch today.**
Cook: **Oh, no you wouldn't.**

Student #1: What's the best thing to have in our school cafeteria?
Student #2: A brown-bag lunch.

The food in our school cafeteria is so bad the mice order takeout lunches.

What do dance school students drink with their lunches?
Tap water.

How did the plate get a crack in it?
It had a lunch break.

What do you call a young Scot who works in a school cafeteria? The lunch laddie.

Knock! Knock!
Who's there?
Mister E.
Mister E. who
Mister E. meat is what they're serving for lunch today.

What did the Abominable Snowman Lunch Lady serve to her students?
Cold cuts.

Which is the best day of the week to serve hamburgers for lunch?
Fry day.

What did the school bowling team order for lunch?
Spare ribs.

What's a grumpy salad made with? Lettuce alone.

What kind of cheese did the lunch lady serve to the school basketball team?
Swish cheese.

What kind of cake should you never eat for dessert? A cake of soap.

What is a down-to-earth sandwich made of? Ground beef.

What did the geometry teacher have for lunch?
A square meal.

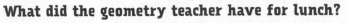

What did the slice of bread say to the sweet roll?
Will you be my honeybun?

What is an author's sandwich made of?
Lots of baloney on write bread.

Where's the worst place to sit in the school cafeteria?
At the cruel kids' table.

What did the tennis player say to the lunch lady?
What are you serving today?

Why did the school principal hire a tightrope walker to prepare lunch?
He wanted her students to have balanced meals.

New Teacher: Do they have good food in the school cafeteria?
Old Teacher: Yes. Until somebody cooks it.

Cook: I'm tired of everyone kidding me about the meals I serve.
Principal: Don't take offense. They're just tasteless jokes.

How did the butter knife get into trouble in the cafeteria?
It kept cutting up at the lunch table.

. . . .

Why did the dumb student eat a five-dollar bill?
His mother told him it was his lunch money.

. . . .

What do you get if you eat your lunch too fast?
A meal ticket.

. . . .

What did the leopard say to the lion when the lunch bell rang?
Save me a spot at our table.

. . . .

Why did the student throw his lunch in the garbage?
It was nothing but junk food.

. . . .

Knock! Knock!
Who's there?
Sieve.
Sieve who?
Sieve me a seat in the lunchroom.

. . . .

What did the Drivers' Ed teacher have for lunch?
Park chops.

. . . .

What did the math teachers do in the cafeteria?
They divided their lunches among them.

Student: For crying out loud! Are we having alphabet soup for lunch again?

Lunch Lady: Yes. Read it and weep.

- -

Why did the dog go to school at noon?

He was part of the flea lunch program.

- -

Why was the math teacher overweight?

Every day at lunch he added a few pounds.

- -

Why did the student bring scissors into the cafeteria?

He wanted to cut the lunch line.

- -

Boy: Does this cafeteria food taste as bad as it looks?

Girl: No. It tastes worse.

- -

Knock! Knock!

Who's there?

Hiatus.

Hiatus who?

Hiatus lunch and now the school bully is after me.

- -

Lunch Lady: **Why do you have a pickle behind your ear?**

Dork Student: **Oh no! I must have eaten my pencil!**

Smart Alecks

Teacher: Richard, find North America on the wall map.
Richard: There it is.
Teacher: Correct. Now class, who discovered North America.
Class: Richard!

....

Principal: Don't you enjoy going to school?
Debbie: Of course I enjoy going to school. It's the being there that bugs me!

....

Teacher: What do you want to get out of high school?
Student: I just want to get out.

....

Teacher: How would you find the square root of 144?
Student: I'd ask the kid sitting next to me.

....

Teacher: Robert, did you miss school yesterday?
Robert: No way! I didn't miss it one bit.

....

Teacher: Why aren't you using your pencil to take the exam?
Student: It's pointless.

....

Teacher: What are you laughing at, Henry?
Henry: Sorry, teacher. I was just thinking of something funny.
Teacher: From now on when you're in my class, don't think.

Teacher: How would you feed twenty people with ten apples?
Girl: Make applesauce.

Principal: Why don't you ever take any books home?
Boy: Because they're school books not home books.

....

Teacher: What can you tell me about the English Channel?
Boy: Nothing. We don't have satellite TV.

Principal: Do you come to school just to make trouble?
Bully: No. I also like recess, lunch, and gym.

....

Teacher: Do you know what the word extinct means?
Student: It means a skunk died.

....

Bob: What are you going to do during your summer vacation?
Rob: I'm going to review everything I learned in school the past year.
Bob: And what are you going to do on the second day of vacation?

....

Teacher: Take a seat. Rupert.
Rupert: Where do you want me to take it, teacher?

....

Teacher: Morgan, what do you consider to be the most important date in history?
Morgan: June 28th.
Teacher: What's so special about June 28th?
Morgan: It's my birthday.

....

Principal: Why are you always a perfect idiot?
Student: Everyone is good at something, and I also practice a lot.

Girl: Let's play school. I'll be the teacher.

Boy: Okay. I'll be absent.

....

Mom: Why is your report card soaking wet?

Son: Because all of my grades are below C-level.

....

Teacher: James! I'm happy to see that you've finally raised your hand.

James: Thank you teacher. Now, can I go to the bathroom?

....

Father: Gah! You flunked every class.

Boy: Well, I might not be smart, but at least I'm consistent.

....

Teacher: Does anyone know the name of the First Lady?

Girl: Eve.

....

Teacher: How long did Thomas Edison live?

Boy: He lived until he died.

....

Mom: Summer vacation is not the time to stop learning.

Son: Right. I did that the week before school ended.

Principal: You were late every day this week.

Student: That's not true. I was only late four times. The other day I played hooky.

....

Girl: Why don't you like history class?

Boy: It's always the same old story.

....

Teacher: Neatness counts on the test you just took, class.

Maggie: In that case, I should get a good grade. My paper doesn't have a mark on it.

Instructor: What's the most common cause of dry skin?

Medical student: Towels.

Father: Why do you hate the first day of school so much?

Son: Because it's followed by the second day of school and the third day and on and on.

....

Mother: Why are your grades so low after Christmas vacation?

Girl: You know how it is, Mom. Everything gets marked down after the holidays.

....

Teacher: What do you know about the Grand Canyon?

Student: It's America's greatest depression.

....

Teacher: How did you like our lesson about the Pacific Ocean?

Student: All of the facts are just starting to sink in.

....

Father: How did you find school today?

Son: It was easy. The bus dropped us off at the main entrance.

....

Teacher: Zeke, name six wild animals that live in Africa.

Zeke: Three lions, two zebras, and a giraffe.

Teacher: What comes before March?

Military Student: Forward.

....

Music Student: What are those papers the orchestra leader is looking at?

Music Teacher: That's the score.

Music Student: Oh. Who won?

....

Girl: I know English good.

Boy: I know English "well."

Girl: Then I guess we'll both do okay on the exam.

....

Girl: That's Mr. Smith. He wants to be a member of the school board.

Boy: I'm already a member.

Girl: What do you mean?

Boy: I'm bored with school.

Mother: What did you learn in school today?
Son: Not much. They expect me to go back for more tomorrow.

Teacher: Class! If you don't stop making all this racket, I'll go crazy.
Student: Too late, Teach. We quieted down ten minutes ago.

Teacher: What did you write your research paper on?
Student: On my laptop.

Teacher: Do you know what procrastination is?
Student: Ask me again later.

Bob: I didn't know anything until I started school.
Rob: Neither did I. And I still don't. But now they test me on it.

Teacher: Would you like to do some addition for me?
Student: I don't have a problem with that.

Mother: How do you like doing homework?
Daughter: I like doing nothing better.

Teacher: Why did you stop referring to that dictionary?
Student: Words no longer have any meaning for me.

Teacher: What do you expect to be when you get out of high school?
Student: Retired.

Teacher: What's a polygon?

Student: Something that eventually turns into a frog.

Teacher: How long does it take you to do your homework?

Student: About two hours ... three if Dad helps me.

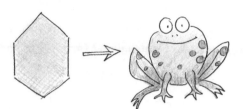

Teacher: Why are you crawling into my classroom?

Student: Because you said anyone who walks in late gets detention.

Student: I don't think I deserved a zero on this exam.

Teacher: I agree, but it's the lowest mark I can give you.

Teacher: What's the difference between one yard and two yards?

Marty: A picket fence.

Robert: Teacher, would you punish me for something I didn't do?

Teacher: Of course not.

Robert: That's good, because I didn't do my homework.

Teacher: Did you think band practice would be nothing but fun?

Student: Yes. I came here to play.

Chemistry Teacher: What do you know about nitrates?

Student: Sometimes they're cheaper than day rates.

Father: I want you to have all of the things I didn't have as a boy.

Son: You mean like "A's" on my report card?

➤ ➤

English Teacher: Have you read much Shakespeare?

Student: No. I'm waiting for his new book to come out.

◀ ◀

Teacher: A noun is a person, place, or thing.

Student: Well, make up your mind. Which is it?

➤ ➤

Teacher: What will you do when you're as big as your father?

Boy: Diet.

◀ ◀

Teacher: Did you know Henry Hudson discovered the Hudson River?

Student: Wow! What a coincidence.

➤ ➤

Teacher: How many feet are there in a yard?

Boy: It depends on how many people are standing in the yard.

◀ ◀

Teacher: Billy Smith, all of the other students in class forgot to do their homework. Did you forget, too?

Billy: No teacher. But tomorrow I'll try harder.

➤ ➤

Teacher: Did your father write this composition for you, Marty?

Marty: No teacher. He started it, but my mom had to write the whole thing over.

Teacher: Who was Homer?

Boy: The person Hank Aaron made famous.

◄ ◄

Teacher: Can you tell me how fast light travels?

Boy: I don't know, but it always gets here too early in the morning.

► ►

Boy: I know the capital of North Carolina.

Teacher: Oh, really?

Boy: No. Raleigh.

◄ ◄ ◄ ◄ ◄ ◄ ◄ ◄ ◄ ◄ ◄ ◄ ◄ ◄ ◄ ◄ ◄ ◄ ◄ ◄

Sunday School Teacher: **The Three Wise Men followed a big star.**

Boy: **Oh! They were like biblical paparazzi.**

► ►

Teacher: Michelangelo painted the Sistine Chapel on his back. Isn't that amazing?

Boy: Big Deal. My uncle is a sailor and he had a battleship tattooed on his chest.

◄ ◄ ◄ ◄ ◄ ◄ ◄ ◄ ◄ ◄ ◄ ◄ ◄

Teacher: I heard you went to the Grand Canyon on vacation. What did you think of it?

Girl: It was just gorges.

► ► ► ► ► ► ► ► ► ► ► ► ►

Teacher: Does anyone know Samuel Clemens' pen name?

Boy: No. And we don't know the name of his pencil either.

CHAPTER 3

MONSTER MIRTH!

Monster 1: I just devoured a gym teacher, a fitness expert, and an aerobics instructor.

Monster 2: Gosh! You sure eat a lot of health food.

. . . .

Where do you go to gas up a monster truck?

To a villain station.

. . . .

Monster 1: Last night I had my new neighbors for dinner.

Monster 2: How was the meal?

Monster 1: Great! They were delicious.

. . . .

Why does Frankenstein walk funny?

Monster wedgie.

. . . .

Why did the Frankenstein Monster go to a psychiatrist?

He thought he had a screw loose.

. . . .

Why did Dr. Cyclops close his ophthalmology school?

He only had one pupil.

. . . .

Who do you call to clean a filthy haunted house?

The Ghost Dusters.

. . . .

Ghostbuster: How much will you charge to haunt my boss?

Ghost: For ten bucks I'll scare the wits out of him.

Ghostbuster: Here's five dollars to do the job. My boss is a half-wit.

. . . .

What do you get if you cross hot oil with a wizard?

A frying sorcerer.

What do you feed a baby witch?
A magic formula.

....

what's ten feet tall, creepy, and glows?
The Frankenshine Monster.

....

NOTICE: Boris the Hangman always watches the nightly noose report.

....

Knock! Knock!
Who's there?
Logan.
Logan who?
Logan see if there's a full moon out.

....

Knock! Knock!
Who's there?
Zelda.
Zelda who?
Zelda house! I think it's haunted.

....

NOTICE: Big Foot drives a monster toe truck.

....

What did Godzilla say when he saw a NASCAR race?
Oh boy! Fast food.

....

Why did the Invisible Woman go to the beauty parlor?
Her hair had no body at all.

Harry: I'm tired of studying magic.
Wizard: Maybe you should rest a spell.

....

What's ghastly and cleans floors?
The Grim Sweeper.

....

Who haunts the chicken coop?
The Grim Peeper.

....

Knock! Knock!
Who's there?
I scream.
I scream who?
I scream tastes cool on a hot day.

....

Igor: Where did you learn to write horror stories?
Boris: In a little red ghoul house.

Why did Baby Frankenstein ask so many questions?

After the Mad Doctor charged him up, he was full of watts.

....

Why did Little Frankenstein go to the playground?

He wanted to ride the scary-go-round.

....

Show me a very sophisticated witch ... and I'll show you a charm school graduate.

....

Knock! Knock!
Who's there?
Weaver.
Weaver who?
Weaver alone, you horrible monster!

....

Which dinosaur likes to play golf?
Tee Rex.

....

What feat did the ghoul gymnast perform?

He did a cemetery vault.

....

Why was the Egyptian pharaoh in a time-out chair?

He disobeyed his mummy.

....

KOOKY QUESTION: **Do witches and wizards participate in spelling bees?**

What did Dr. Frankenstein say to his exhausted monster?

Lie down. You're in for a shock.

....

Why did the tough little ghosts get detention after school?

They were frighting at recess.

....

What weapon does Indiana Bones carry?

A boo whip.

....

Where is the best place to bury a monster?

In a fiendish plot.

....

What did the ghoul say when he saw a new grave?

Yo! I can dig it.

KOOKY QUESTION: Do monsters wear ghoulashes on rainy days?

Why did the ghost go to the pond?
He was a duck haunter.

NOTICE: Most ghosts like spiritual music.

Boris: Uh-oh! The Invisible Man is taking a shower.
Lady Monster: EEK!
Boris: Relax. There's nothing to see.

What kind of evergreen trees grow in Transylvania?
Frankenpine monsters.

Artifact Dealer: Would you like to purchase an Egyptian mummy?
Customer: Yes. And could you gift-wrap it.

What do you get if you cross Bambi with a ghost?
Bamboo.

What's green, slimy, and scares people?
Kermit the Boo-Frog.

What do you call a ghost who tracks down elephants and rhinos?
A big-game haunter.

NOTICE: Never lend money to the Invisible Man.
He'll disappear with your cash.

What do you get if you cross a fisherman with Harry Potter?
Someone who knows how to cast spells.

What do you get if you cross a ghost with a rodent?
A haunted mouse.

What's creepy, clingy, and green?
The Frankenvine Monster.

Knock! Knock!
Who's there?
Shepherd.
Shepherd who?
Shepherd a monster outside.

NOTICE: Fashionable ghosts wear designer boo jeans.

Why doesn't death ever miss a phone call?
He has a grim beeper.

Why did Godzilla eat a volcano?
He wanted a hot lunch.

Why did Godzilla devour the Eiffel Tower?
He was in the mood for French food.

Why did Godzilla consume Alaska?
He wanted a cold supper.

ATTENTION: When Godzilla travels to Great Britain, he eats fish and ships.

▶ ▶ ▶ ▶ ▶ ▶ ▶ ▶ ▶ ▶ ▶ ▶ ▶ ▶ ▶ ▶ ▶ ▶ ▶ ▶

How do you measure a cemetery?
Use a graveyard stick.

◀ ◀ ◀ ◀ ◀ ◀ ◀ ◀ ◀ ◀ ◀ ◀ ◀ ◀ ◀ ◀ ◀ ◀ ◀

Who cleans up a dirty dungeon?
The torture chambermaid.

▶ ▶ ▶ ▶ ▶ ▶ ▶ ▶ ▶ ▶ ▶ ▶ ▶ ▶ ▶ ▶ ▶ ▶ ▶ ▶

Ivan: We'll have to do something about the hot-tempered monster you created.

Mad Doctor: Why?

Ivan: It keeps losing its head.

◀ ◀ ◀ ◀ ◀ ◀ ◀ ◀ ◀ ◀ ◀ ◀ ◀

Which letter of the alphabet turns into a monster when the full moon rises?
The Evil I.

▶ ▶ ▶ ▶ ▶ ▶ ▶ ▶ ▶ ▶ ▶ ▶ ▶

Knock! Knock!
Who's there?
Eerie.
Eerie who?
Eerie go again!

◀ ◀ ◀ ◀ ◀ ◀ ◀ ◀ ◀ ◀ ◀ ◀ ◀ ◀ ◀ ◀ ◀ ◀

Mad Doctor: How can I create monsters if I have no parts to work with?
Boris: Don't blame me if you're having an out-of-bodies experience.

▶ ▶ ▶ ▶ ▶ ▶ ▶ ▶ ▶ ▶ ▶ ▶ ▶ ▶ ▶ ▶ ▶ ▶ ▶

Where does the Abominable Snowman hide his secret money?
In a slush fund.

What is a yeti's biggest medical problem?
Cold sores.

What does a yeti put in his coffee?
Cold cream.

What did the yeti say when he found a frozen Roman soldier?
Oh boy! Italian ice.

How does Godzilla buy things at the undersea mall when he's out of cash?
He uses a depth charge card.

Why did Godzilla eat the burning apartment building?
He likes home cooking.

What did the people say after Godzilla devoured their apartment building?
That beast ate us out of house and home.

What does the Frankenstein Monster do when he runs short of energy?
He uses his monster charge card.

What did Godzilla say after he ate a dozen armored vehicles?
Tanks for dinner.

Why did Godzilla eat Fort Knox?
He wanted an after-dinner mint.

Where do monsters go to buy a used car?
In the Boris Car Lot.

Knock! Knock!
Who's there?
Karlof.
Karlof who?
Karlof your dogs, monster hunters. I surrender.

·····································

Boris: I know a girl named Wanda who can cast spells.
Igor: Gee, she must be a magic Wanda.

·····································

What creature did Mad Dr. Cheese invent?
The Frankenstein Muenster.

·····································

Mad Doctor: **Yesterday I created a rope monster.**
Igor: **Did knot!**

·····································

Monster: My fingers don't work right.
Mad Scientist: I knew I shouldn't have used second-hand parts when I made you.

·····································

Vampire: **Hello, stranger. Where are you from?**
Frankenstein Monster: **Parts of me are from New York, Texas, Ohio, Maine, Alabama, New Jersey, and other places.**
Vampire: **Wow, you're a real all-American guy.**

·····································

Movie Director: Your metal robot monster is too nice.
Mad Doctor: Can I help it if he has a heart of gold?

·····································

What is the Abominable Snowman's favorite treat?
Snowcones.

·····································

What kind of craft does a space ghost fly?
A BOO-F-O.

How do you clean a dirty space monster?
Chase it through a meteor shower.

. . . .

Which sea serpent is very sloppy?

The Loch Mess Monster.

. . . .

Invisible Man: I'm sick, Doc. I have a skin rash.
Mad Doctor: Don't worry. I'll clear it up.

. . . .

Psychologist: Why are you sad, Ms. Skeleton?
Ms. Skeleton: I have no body to love.

. . . .

What kind of candy do mummies eat after dinner?
Parch-mints.

. . . .

Which mummy has a static problem with his wrapping?

Cling Tut.

. . . .

Boris: That corn plant only grows when it's dark out.
Ivan: Maybe it's a night stalker.

. . . .

What do you get if you cross a ghoul with a cobbler?

A creep shoe.

. . . .

Why did the mummy wear a kilt and carry bagpipes?
Because he was Scotch taped.

. . . .

Mad Scientist: I plan to create a giant rabbit monster.
Igor: Humph! Now that's a hare-brained scheme.

Knock! Knock!
Who's there?
Egypt.
Egypt who?
Egypt me when he sold me this phony magic potion.

NOTICE: Dr. Frankenstein overcharged his monster for his operation.

FRANKENSTEIN FRIGHT SIGHTINGS:

Beware! Here comes the Frankenpine Monsters and there's tree of them.

Beware! Here comes the Frankensty Monster and he's going hog wild.

Beware! Here comes the Frankensteam Monster and he's boiling mad.

Beware! Here comes the Frankenstair Monster and he's climbing up to get us.

Pat: I just saw a horror movie about a monster Leprechaun.
Matt: Lucky you.

What kind of vegetables do monsters eat?
Human beans.

Knock! Knock!
Who's there?
Ooze.
Ooze who?
Ooze afraid of monsters? Not me!

What is a monster baseball player's favorite movie?
The Scary Pitcher Show.

Which mummy was a football quarterback?
King Hut!

Boy Ghost: What game do you want to play?
Girl Ghost: Hide and shriek!

How do you make a gingerbread monster?
Use weird dough.

Knock! Knock!
Who's there?
Weird.
Weird who?
Weird you hide the monster you made last night?

Knock! Knock!
Who's there?
Wail.
Wail who?
Wail find your monster if we have to search every inch of your castle.

Godzilla eats real submarine sandwiches.
Vampires hate stake dinners.

Boris: I penned a horror story about an axe murderer.
Ivan: Big deal. So now you're a hack writer.

Knock! Knock!
Who's there?
Talon.
Talon who?
Talon monster stories scares little kids.

Knock! Knock!
Who's there?
I'm Gladys.
I'm Gladys who?
I'm Gladys spooky story is finally over.

NOTICE: The old mystic bank has fortune tellers.

Why did the monster go to the hospital?
To have his ghoulstones removed.

Why don't ghosts star in cowboy movies?
Because they always spook the horses.

Knock! Knock!
Who's there?
Ditty.
Ditty who?
Ditty see a monster outside or not?

Knock! Knock!
Who's there?
Sheena.
Sheena who?
Have you Sheena big ugly monster around here?

Monster #1: Grr! I'm really angry. The Mad Doctor who created me forgot to give me a brain transplant.

Monster #2: Calm down and I'll give you a piece of my mind.

What do you get if you cross Sasquatch with a centipede.
A big foot, foot, foot, foot, foot, foot.

What's the first sounds you hear after Godzilla sees a flock of turkeys?
Gobble! Gobble!

What does Godzilla do when he sees a flock of geese?
Chow down.

What does a creepy person get when he learns to fly?
A high ghoul diploma.

Which creepy general was the victor of the monsters' civil war?
Gholysses S. Grant.

Boy: How did you get a role in that new ghost movie?
Girl: I did well in the scream test.

How did the ghost keep his haunted house?
In a frightful mess.

What do you get if you cross a dinosaur with the ruler of the Emerald City?
The Giant Lizard of Oz.

Which dinosaur loves to wear plaid clothing?

Tyrannosaurus Chex.

What makes dinosaurs itch and scratch?

A fleahistoric bug.

Who is the biggest dinosaur musician?

The Raptor.

What do you get if you cross a wild horse with a dinosaur?

A Broncosaurus.

Yeti: Did you date the Abominable Snowgirl?

Sasquatch: No. I asked her out, but she gave me the cold shoulder.

Witch: The stick of my magic broom is broken.

Wizard: Don't worry, I'll handle it.

Ghost pirate: How will I know where the treasure is buried?

Sea witch: That's easy. Hex marks the spot.

What kind of horse does a cowboy ghost ride?

A night mare.

Knock! Knock!

Who's there?

Wilma.

Wilma who?

Wilma howling keep you awake all night?

Mother Witch to Daughter: If you don't study hard at charm school, you'll never learn to spell correctly.

What kind of weapon does a witch from space use?

A hex-ray gun.

What do you get when you cross cheddar cheese with a sorcerer?

Cheese Whiz.

Where's the best place for a mummy to live?

In an old, old, old, old, old age home.

....

What do ghosts eat with roast beef and gravy?

Monster mash potatoes.

....

Why didn't the mummy take a vacation?

He was wrapped up in his work.

....

What does a construction ghost drive?

A boodozer.

....

What does BFF mean to a monster?

Beast Friends Forever.

....

What kind of novels does the Abominable Snowman write?

Chilling tales of suspense.

....

What does a yeti grow in his Himalayan garden?

Llama beans.

....

How does a dumb monster count up to fifteen?

It uses its fingers.

Dracula: I'll see you later.
Invisible Man: No you won't.

....

What zombie makes marital arts movies?

Dead Lee.

....

How do you produce a zombie song?

Kill the music.

....

What do you put on a zombie wanted poster?

Wanted Dead or Not Alive.

....

Where does a zombie keep a skeleton bird?

In a rib cage.

Vampires

What do you call a two-headed vampire?
A twilight double header.

What do you call Dracula's unruly children?
Vampire brats.

What happened to the vampire grape who got caught out in the sun?
He turned into a raisin.

When does Dracula visit with his children's teachers?
On bat-to-school night.

Vampire: How much did you pay for the lining in the bottom of your coffin?
Dracula: I got it dirt cheap.

Knock! Knock!
Who's there?
Zealous.
Zealous who?
Zealous an amulet to protect us from vampires.

Which vampire flew a kite during a thunderstorm?
Benjamin Fanglin.

When do vampires attack geeks and dweebs?
On dork nights.

Villager 1: Do you think we can burn down Dracula's castle and get away with it?

Villager 2: Yes. But it'll be a torch and go situation.

....

Show me a vampire who loves to play golf ... and I'll show you a monster who enjoys night clubbing.

....

What did Judge Dracula say as he got into his coffin at daybreak?

It's time to close this case.

....

Which vampire whines too much?

Pout Dracula.

....

What does a vampire wear on his head when he flies around?

A batting helmet.

....

How does a gal vampire flirt with a guy vampire?

She bats her eyelashes at him.

....

Igor: **Is Dracula a conceited vampire?**

Boris: **Yes. He's a vein monster.**

....

SIGN ON A VAMPIRE FAST FOOD STORE: Stop in for a quick bite!

....

Why did the school ghoul get her vampire addition problem wrong?

Because she didn't count Dracula.

....

What do you get if you cross Dracula with a cashier?

Count Yourchange.

NOTICE: Vampires who play baseball like to go to batting cages.

Who is Count Dracula's favorite superhero?
Batman.

Boris: Why is that baby vampire chewing on your neck?
Bride of Dracula: He's teething.

Nurse: What is your blood type?
Vampire: I'm not fussy. I'll drink anything.

Who is the leader of the vampire ducks?
Count Down.

Why did the girl go to the doctor after her date with Dracula?
He gave her a sore throat.

Does Dracula like sailboats?
No. But he's very fond of blood vessels.

Villager: We know you sleep in a coffin filled with the soil of your native land.
Dracula: That's a dirty lie!

Igor: I just saw a ten foot vampire.
Boris: Now that's unusual. Most vampires only have two feet.

What do vampire bats order at I-Hop?
Flapjacks.

Where is the most dangerous place to live in Transylvania?
Necks-door to Count Dracula.

NOTICE: Mr. & Mrs. Vampire have undying love for each other.

Knock! Knock!
Who's there?
Dewey.
Dewey who?
Dewey have enough garlic to repel a vampire attack?

What makes an African vampire bat very happy?
Flying into a herd of giraffes.

Why did the vampire bat fly into a cave?
She wanted to hang out with her friends.

What is one job a vampire can never have?
A day laborer.

What do you call two male vampires who
have the same mother?
Blood brothers.

Igor: Why are you doing somersaults?
Vampire: I'm training to be an acro-bat.

What do you call a baby vampire who is too little to walk?
A night crawler.

What do you get if you cross a vampire bat with a pig?
A hampire.

>>>>>>>>>>>>>>>>>>>>>

Which vampire is always on a diet?
Count Calories.

<<<<<<<<<<<<<<<<<<<<<

Where do vampires play tennis?
At a night court.

>>>>>>>>>>>>>>>>>>>>>

Why did the vampire take an art class?
He wanted to learn how to draw blood.

<<<<<<<<<<<<<<<<<<<<<

What do you call a vampire who can stalk victims for twenty-four hours straight?
An all-day sucker.

>>>>>>>>>>>>>>>>>>>>>

NOTICE: Being a vampire is a fly-by-night occupation.

<<<<<<<<<<<<<<<<<<<<<

Knock! Knock!
Who's there?
Welcome.
Welcome who?
Welcome to your rescue if vampires attack.

>>>>>>>>>>>>>>>>

What happened when the clock saw a vampire bat?
It became alarmed.

<<<<<<<<<<<<<<<<

What do you get if you cross a vampire with soda pop?
Count Dracola.

Knock! Knock!
Who's there?
Wheelbarrow.
Wheelbarrow who?
Wheelbarrow your bloodhounds to track down Dracula.

▶ ▶ ▶ ▶ ▶ ▶ ▶ ▶ ▶ ▶ ▶ ▶ ▶ ▶ ▶ ▶ ▶ ▶

NOTICE: When it comes to trusting creatures of the night, never stick your neck out for a vampire.

◀ ◀ ◀ ◀ ◀ ◀ ◀ ◀ ◀ ◀ ◀ ◀ ◀ ◀ ◀ ◀ ◀ ◀

Knock! Knock!
Who's there?
Achoo.
Achoo who?
Achoo on people's necks, said the vampire.

▶ ▶ ▶ ▶ ▶ ▶ ▶ ▶ ▶ ▶ ▶ ▶ ▶ ▶ ▶ ▶ ▶ ▶

What is Santa Vampire's favorite kind of blood?
Type O-O-O.

◀ ◀ ◀ ◀ ◀ ◀ ◀ ◀ ◀ ◀ ◀ ◀ ◀ ◀ ◀ ◀ ◀ ◀

Where do chicken vampires live?
In Hensylvania.

▶ ▶ ▶ ▶ ▶ ▶ ▶ ▶ ▶ ▶ ▶ ▶ ▶ ▶ ▶ ▶ ▶ ▶

NOTICE: **Hobo vampires have been known to hop on fright trains.**

◀ ◀ ◀ ◀ ◀ ◀ ◀ ◀ ◀ ◀ ◀ ◀ ◀ ◀ ◀ ◀ ◀

What do you get if you cross a large bell with a vampire?
A ding bat.

▶ ▶ ▶ ▶ ▶ ▶ ▶ ▶ ▶ ▶ ▶ ▶ ▶ ▶ ▶ ▶ ▶ ▶

What is a baby vampire's favorite game?
Batty-cake.

◀ ◀ ◀ ◀ ◀ ◀ ◀ ◀ ◀ ◀ ◀ ◀ ◀ ◀ ◀ ◀ ◀ ◀

Why did the vampire bite a light bulb?
He wanted brighter teeth.

How do you prove a vampire can turn into a bat?
Give it a fly detector test.

Knock! Knock!
Who's there?
Shirley.
Shirley who?
Shirley you're not afraid of vampires.

Why was the young vampire unhappy?
He needed braces.

Why did Dracula go to the hospital lab?
He wanted to get some blood work.

NOTICE: Actors who always play vampires are blood type cast.

Knock! Knock!
Who's there?
Menu.
Menu who?
Menu see Count Dracula, protect your neck.

What did Dracula ask the vampire?
Are you a blood relative?

What do you get if you cross Dracula with a bad boxer?
Count Meout.

Knock! Knock!
Who's there?
Harold.
Harold who?
Harold is Count Dracula? I bet he's at least one hundred years old.

What do you get if you cross Dracula with Sir Lancelot?
A bite in shining armor.

FLASH! Then there was the dumb vampire who cheated on his blood test.

What did Dracula get when he bit the Abominable Snowman?
Frost bite.

Knock! Knock!
Who's there?
Cheese.
Cheese who?
Cheese kind of cute even if she is a vampire.

What's the fastest way to destroy a vampire?
Use a minute stake.

What's the tallest structure in Transylvania?
The Vampire State Building.

Why doesn't Godzilla eat vampires?
They leave a bat taste in his mouth.

Knock! Knock!
Who's there?
Cement.
Cement who?
Cement to scream when she saw Dracula, but she fainted instead.

What do you call a dead pharaoh lying next to a sleeping vampire?
Mummy and Batty.

Why does Count Dracula use mouthwash?
He has bat breath.

Why did the witch divorce her vampire husband?
The magic had gone out of their relationship.

What is a vampire's favorite game?
Batminton.

What happens when vampires visit
New York City?

They take a bite out of the Big Apple.

NOTICE: Count Dracula is a graduate of night school.

> **Reporter:** Do you like playing vampires in every movie you make?
>
> **Actor:** Yes. Acting's in my blood.

What did the mother vampire tell the baby vampire at meal time?

Take little bites.

NOTICE: Dracula has a bat reputation.

What are the two things Dracula takes with him when he travels light?

His casket and his toothbrush.

> **Werewolf:** I just insured key parts of my body. See this clawed hand. It's insured for a thousand dollars.
>
> **Vampire:** Wow! So that's your grand paw!

Why did the vampire climb out on the barn roof?

To get to the weather vein.

FLASH! Count Dracula's victim walked off the set of a big horror movie because the director only gave her a bit part.

What do you get if you cross a vampire with a Brontosaurus?
A monster that sleeps in the biggest coffin you ever saw.

....

What's the most dangerous job in Transylvania?
Being Dracula's orthodontist.

....

Why did Dracula pal around with Frankenstein?
He wanted a friend he could look up to.

....

Knock! Knock!
Who's there?
Vein.
Vein who?
Vein you go to Dracula's castle be sure to wear garlic around your neck.

....

Why did Dracula run out of the garden?
He saw sunflowers coming up.

....

knock! knock!
who's there?
Doughnut.
Doughnut who?
Doughnut go to
Dracula's castle
after sunset.

....

**What did the
vampire have for
dessert?**

Veinilla ice
cream.

What's the difference between a senior citizen and an old vampire?
At night a senior citizen's teeth come out and that's when an old vampire's teeth go in.

Where does hypnotist Dracula live?
In Trancelvania.

Why did the vampire join the circus?
He wanted to be a jugular.

What month does Count Dracula like least?
Noveinber.

Zack: Did you hear the joke about Dracula's teeth?
Mack: No.
Zack: Never mind. You wouldn't get the point.

Knock! Knock!
Who's there?
Lena.
Lena who?
Lena little closer. I want to bite your neck.

* COUGH *
* COUGH *

Why is the vampire family so close?
Because blood is thicker than water.

Why did Dracula take cough medicine?
To stop his coffin.

Son: Mom, am I really a vampire?
Mother: We'll talk about that later, son. The sun is rising. Now close your coffin and go to sleep.

What do you get if you cross a giant vampire with a hairy beast?
A big bat wolf.

....

What kind of soup does a vampire eat?
Alpha-bat soup.

....

Zombies

What's another name for Attila the Zombie?
The Hun-Dead.

....

Where do zombies go swimming?
In the Dead Sea.

....

What did one zombie say to the other?
We're a dying breed.

....

Why did Mrs. Zombie join a monster health club?
She was starting to lose her ghoulish figure.

....

Boris: Does Mrs. Zombie's wedding ring have a diamond in it?

Igor: No. It has a tombstone.

Why was Mr. Zombie so carefree?
He never had to worry about cost-of-living expenses.

What did the boy zombie say to the pretty girl zombie?
I've been dying to go out with you.

What did the zombie say to the funny comedian?
Stop! Your jokes are killing me.

When did the phone turn into a zombie?
After the line went dead.

What's the worst job to have in zombie land?
Selling life insurance.

What did one zombie surfer say to the other zombie surfer?
Get a life, dude!

What do male zombies splash on their faces when they wake up?
After grave lotion.

Zombie #1: **You look exhausted.**
Zombie #2: **I'm so tired I'm dead on my feet.**

What game do zombie kids like to play?
Corpse and robbers.

How did the zombie make his house burglar-proof?
He put deadbolt locks on all the doors.

What's one thing a zombie can never be at a social gathering?

The life of the party.

. . . .

ATTENTION: Zombie pirate captain needs a skeleton crew to sail his ghost ship.

. . . .

Boy Zombie: **If you don't go out with me, I'll just die.**

Girl Zombie: **It's a little late for that.**

. . . .

NOTICE: Zombie appliances don't come with a lifetime guarantee.

. . . .

Monster Hunter: For your crimes, Mr. Zombie, we plan to rebury you.

Zombie: Humph! Don't think I'm going to accept this punishment lying down.

. . . .

What position did the zombie play on the football team?

Dead end.

. . . .

Where did the zombie finish in the foot race?

Dead last.

. . . .

Where did the zombie family go camping?

In Death Valley.

DEFINITION: Zombie — a person with a bad life-insurance policy.

. . . .

Why can't a zombie write an autobiography?

He has no life story.

. . . .

What's one thing you never find in the home of a zombie?

Living-room furniture.

. . . .

Why did the zombie go to a psychologist?

He had grave problems.

What happens when a zombie graduates from college?

Everyone mourns his passing.

....

When did the watch maker become a zombie?

When his time was up.

....

When did John Deere become a zombie?

When he bought the farm.

....

When did the fisherman become a zombie?

When he reached the end of the line.

....

What do you get if you cross a snail with a zombie?

Slow death.

....

What do you get if you cross zombies with a library.

Dead silence.

....

Where do zombies reside?

On dead end streets.

....

What did the zombie say to the judge at the end of his trial?

Please, your honor, give me a life sentence.

Knock! Knock!

Who's there?

Zombies.

Zombies who?

Zombies gather honey while others guard the hive.

....

NOTICE: Zombie actors refuse to perform in front of a live audience.

....

What did the zombie say when a voodoo witch doctor jumped out of the shadows?

Gosh! You scared the life out of me.

....

When did the hairdresser become a zombie?

After she dyed.

When did the quarterback become a zombie?
After he kicked off.

When did the frogman become a zombie?
After he croaked.

When did the door maker become a zombie?
After he got knocked off.

When did the basketball player become a zombie?
After he passed.

When did the cowboy become a zombie?
After the last roundup.

When did the jogger become a zombie?
After his final race was run.

When did the desk clerk become a zombie?
After he checked out for the last time.

Ghoul: Are you going to that new horror play?
Zombie: No. I wouldn't be caught dead in the audience.

Artist #1: I'd like to paint a zombie.
Artist #2: Why risk having a brush with death?

Igor: Is that a zombie goose?
Boris: No. It's just a dead duck.

Why couldn't the zombie go for a boat ride?
He refused to wear a life jacket.

Mad Doctor: Is there a law against creating zombies?
Policeman: Yes. And there's a stiff penalty for breaking it.

Actor: I'm playing a zombie in a horror movie.
Actress: Is it a difficult part?
Actor: Most definitely. This part will be the death of me for sure.

Knock! Knock!
Who's there?
Candice.
Candice who?
Candice zombie be brought back to life?

What do you find under the hood of a zombie car?
A very dead battery.

**Why did the zombie drummer get kicked out
of the band?**
He was a dead beat.

What did the angry father zombie say to his teenage son zombie?
You're totally grounded!

When did the warranty become a zombie?
After it expired.

Why did the zombie go to a doctor?
He was as pale as a ghost.

Why didn't the zombie enlist in the military?
He had no life to give for his country.

Who turned Attila into a zombie?
An evil Hundertaker.

► ►

Why do zombie couples never divorce?
They stay married till death do they part.

◄ ◄

What did the coach shout to his team of zombies?
Hey! Show a little life on the field.

► ►

What do you call a band of thankful zombies?
The Grateful Un-dead.

◄ ◄

Knock! Knock!
Who's there?
It's a waffle.
It's a waffle who?
It's a waffle sight to see zombies walking around.

► ►

Why was the tiny zombie so unhappy?
He had such a short lifespan.

◄ ◄

What is a zombie's favorite play?
Death of a Salesman.

► ►

Why don't zombies tell stories?
Because dead men tell no tales.

◄ ◄

Zombie Desk Clerk: Monsters live on every floor of this hotel.
Vampire: How nice. This place is full of horror stories.

► ►

Where did the zombie work at the post office?
In the dead letter department.

Nurse: Should I put this zombie patient on life support?
Doctor: You're joking right?
Nurse: No, I'm dead serious.

▶ ▶ ▶ ▶ ▶ ▶ ▶ ▶ ▶ ▶ ▶ ▶ ▶ ▶ ▶ ▶

Knock! Knock!
Who's there?
I'm Cher.
I'm Cher who?
I'm Cher afraid of zombies.

◀ ◀ ◀ ◀ ◀ ◀ ◀ ◀ ◀ ◀ ◀ ◀ ◀ ◀ ◀ ◀

What is a zombie's favorite sport?
Hearseback riding.

▶ ▶ ▶ ▶ ▶ ▶ ▶ ▶ ▶ ▶ ▶ ▶ ▶ ▶ ▶ ▶

DAFFY DEFINITION:

Zombie Library — a place that is deadly silent.

◀ ◀ ◀ ◀ ◀ ◀ ◀ ◀ ◀ ◀ ◀ ◀ ◀ ◀ ◀ ◀

Who did the zombie invite to his big party?
All of the guests he could dig up.

▶ ▶ ▶ ▶ ▶ ▶ ▶ ▶ ▶ ▶ ▶ ▶ ▶ ▶ ▶ ▶

What did the Wild West zombie say to the cowboy?
Bury me not on the lone prairie.

◀ ◀ ◀ ◀ ◀ ◀ ◀ ◀ ◀ ◀ ◀ ◀

Why couldn't the zombie keep a secret?
She was dying to tell someone.

▶ ▶ ▶ ▶ ▶ ▶ ▶ ▶ ▶ ▶ ▶ ▶

What do you call a contest that awards zombies as prizes?
A dead giveaway.

"Psssst"

What did the surfer say as he watched the werewolf run away?
Hairy back, dude!

When do werewolves act silly?
When the fool moon rises.

When does a werewolf feel depressed?
Once in a blue moon.

How did the Wolfman get to be a CEO?
He clawed his way to the top.

SIGN ON A CLOSED WEREWOLF STORE:
Dog gone for the day.

How many parents does the Wolfman have?
One maw and four paws.

Knock! Knock!
Who's there?
Wendy.
Wendy who?
Wendy full moon rises, werewolves start to prowl around.

What should you use when you change a baby werewolf's diaper?
Flea powder.

Where do you store wolfmen?

In a werehouse.

. . . .

Knock! Knock!

Who's there?

Obscene.

Obscene who?

Obscene men change into wolves when the full moon rises.

. . . .

WANTED: Horror writer needed to pen hair-raising tales for bald werewolf.

. . . .

What do you get if you cross King Kong with a werewolf?

A giant, very hairy beast that goes ape when the full moon rises.

. . . .

When does the Wolfman turn into a two-bit monster?

When the quarter moon rises.

. . . .

DAFFY DEFINITION: Werewolf—a haunting dog gone wild.

. . . .

Knock! Knock!

Who's there?

Voodoo.

Voodoo who?

Voodoo you think is more dangerous, Dracula or Wolfman?

. . . .

Knock! Knock!

Who's there?

Decry.

Decry who?

Decry of the Wolfman sends shivers down my spine.

Wolfman: Who gave you that bad scratch on your face?
Wolfboy: Nobody gave it to me. I had to fight for it.

Poodle: I turn into a wolf when the full moon rises.
Spaniel: That's just a doggie brag.

ATTENTION: The Wolfman entered a midnight marathon so he could run with the pack.

NOTICE: Werewolves often have hair-brained ideas.

Psychologist: Why are you so depressed, Mr. Zombie?
Mr. Zombie: I have no life.

What do you call a metric werewolf?
The liter of the pack.

What did the shoe salesman say to the Wolfman?
What size do you wear, wolf?

What do you call an athletic werewolf?
A sports cur.

Monster Barber: Why do you always come in for a haircut when the moon is full?
Wolfman: That way I'm sure to get my money's worth.

Dracula: Tonight there's a full moon. Tomorrow there isn't.
Wolfman: Oh well. Hair today. Gone tomorrow.

What do you get if you cross the Wolfman with Santa Claus?
You get a furry Merry Christmas.

What do you get if you cross a lumberjack with the Wolfman?
A timberwolf.

Who prevents forest fires and attacks campers when the moon is full?
Smokey the Bearwolf.

Knock! Knock!
Who's there?
Defer.
Defer who?
Defer coat of a werewolf is very thick.

NOTICE: A werewolf who squeals on his friends is a pack rat.

Knock! Knock!
Who's there?
Eyelid.
Eyelid who?
Eyelid a secret life as a werewolf.

What do you get if you cross Kris Kringle with the Wolfman?
Santa Claws.

Knock! Knock!
Who's there?
Dozen.
Dozen who?
Dozen anyone believe I was chased by a werewolf?

Why did the Wolfman wear torn pants and a ripped shirt?
Because he was dressed to kill.

What did Mrs. Werewolf say to Mr. Werewolf during their argument?
Don't snap at me.

Knock! Knock!
Who's there?
Hubie.
Hubie who?
Hubie in before the full moon rises or a werewolf might get you.

What do you call a bunch of funny werewolves?
A pack of real cards.

Show me a wolfman about to be married...and
I'll show you a dog groomer.

NOTICE: The Wolfman moonlights at a second job.

Which werewolf works for the post office?
The Alpha mail carrier.

How do you get 100 werewolves
in a tiny room?
Pack 'em in.

Who chases the Three Little Pigs when
the moon is full?
The Big Bad Werewolf.

What kind of werewolf goes on hikes and does good deeds?
A wolf cub scout.

What do you get if you cross the Wolfman with a lobster?
I don't know, but you should see the claws on that thing.

Title of Transylvanian Fairy Tale: "The Boy Who Cried Werewolf."

Why do werewolves make bad pets?
They always bite the hand that feeds them.

Oh, My!

NOTICE: Most ghouls work the graveyard shift.

Mad Dr. Morgon: My new monster stands ten feet tall. I named the creature "If."
Gorgon: Gosh! That's a mighty big If.

What happened when the angry villagers trapped the monster orange?
They beat it to a pulp!

Invisible Man: Why won't you give me the lead role in your new horror movie?
Director: Sorry, but I just can't see you in the part.

Knock! Knock!
Who's there?
Dragon.
Dragon who?
Dragon your feet will get your shoes dirty.

What do you call a ghost who haunts a hotel?

An Inn spectre.

....

Knock! Knock!

Who's there?

Clara.

Clara who?

Clara path! Here's comes a monster and I'm out of here!

....

Knock! Knock!

Who's there?

Teller.

Teller who?

Teller to scream loud if she sees a monster.

....

What did the monster say to the alphabet?

I've come to eat U.

Knock! Knock!

Who's there?

Hour.

Hour who?

Hour we going to destroy that monster?

....

What's the best way to view a horror movie?

Watch it on a wide-scream TV.

....

Knock! Knock!

Who's there?

Barn.

Barn who?

Barn down Frankenstein's castle.

....

Knock! Knock!

Who's there?

Gargoyle.

Gargoyle who?

Gargoyle with mouthwash. You have bat breath.

....

KOOKY QUESTION: **Do witch computers have spell check?**

....

CRAZY QUOTE: Great men are made not born. —Dr. Frankenstein.

"Booo!"

Why did the ghosts go to the baseball game?

To boo the umpire.

....

What does a yeti ride?

An Abominable Snowmobile.

....

What do you get if you cross the Ice Age with a witch?

A long cold spell.

....

What happens if you don't pay your exorcist on time?

You get repossessed.

....

How did the witch teacher grade her pupils' spelling tests?

She used a magic marker.

....

What do you get if you cross a witch doctor with morning mist?

Voodew.

Knock! Knock!

Who's there?

Witch Doctor.

Witch Doctor who?

Witch Doctor do you recommend for this operation?

....

What giant ape writes horror stories?

Stephen King Kong.

....

Did you hear about the sea monster that had whale-to-whale carpeting in his house?

....

What do baby ghosts wear on their feet?

Booties.

....

What do you call a spirit who washes dishes?

A ghost busser.

....

Who is spooky and haunts Mother Goose Land?

Little Boo Peep.

....

What happens when a little ghost falls down at the playground?

He gets a boo-boo.

What is a creep's favorite holiday?
April Ghoul's Day.

Knock! Knock!
Who's there?
Icy.
Icy who?
Icy a monster hiding in the bushes.

Abominable Snowman: **Who's paying the check for dinner?**
Sasquatch: **Don't worry. I'll foot the bill.**

What did the ghost driver do when the traffic light turned red?
He screeched to a stop.

Who is spooky and lives under the sea?
Sponge Blob Scare Pants.

What do skeleton students do before exams?
They bone up on their studies.

Knock! Knock!
Who's there?
Alp!
Alp who?
Alp me. A yeti is after me.

YOU TELL 'EM:
You tell 'em palm reader, I'll give you a hand.
You tell 'em Abominable Snowman and state the cold, hard facts.

Knock! Knock!
Who's there?
Candy.
Candy who?
Candy monster you created breathe fire?

Why did King Kong Bunny fall off of the Empire State Building?
The hare planes got him.

What did the witch say to the people of Salem, Massachusetts?
You folks really burn me up.

What do you find in a haunted green house?
Bootiful flowers.
Unholy ground.
Poison Ivy.
Morning Gory Flowers.
Man-eating plants.
Wolfbane.
Crab Grass.

What colors are the ghost flag of America?
Red, white, and boooo!

What do you call a monster gopher?
A ghoul digger.

What do you call a sloppy Sasquatch?
The messing link.

What do you get if you cross an evil woman who casts magic spells with corroded metal?
The Wicked Witch of the Rust.

▶ ▶ ▶ ▶ ▶ ▶ ▶ ▶ ▶ ▶ ▶ ▶ ▶ ▶ ▶ ▶ ▶ ▶ ▶ ▶

What do you call a ghoul protest?
A demon-stration.

◀ ◀ ◀ ◀ ◀ ◀ ◀ ◀ ◀ ◀ ◀ ◀ ◀ ◀ ◀ ◀ ◀ ◀ ◀ ◀

Which monster is a pig farmer?
The Frankenslop monster.

▶ ▶ ▶ ▶ ▶ ▶ ▶ ▶ ▶ ▶ ▶ ▶ ▶ ▶ ▶ ▶ ▶ ▶ ▶ ▶

What do you get if you cross a ghost and a small purple flower?
A shrieking violet.

◀ ◀ ◀ ◀ ◀ ◀ ◀ ◀ ◀ ◀ ◀ ◀ ◀ ◀ ◀ ◀ ◀ ◀ ◀ ◀

Mad Doctor: I made a monster out of an old locomotive. It has a head full of steam.
Igor: Don't forget to attach its engine ears.

▶ ▶ ▶ ▶ ▶ ▶ ▶ ▶ ▶ ▶ ▶ ▶ ▶ ▶ ▶ ▶ ▶ ▶ ▶ ▶

Zelda: I know a hexed number.
Nelda: Witch one?
Zelda: That's right.

◀ ◀ ◀ ◀ ◀ ◀ ◀ ◀ ◀ ◀ ◀ ◀ ◀ ◀ ◀ ◀ ◀ ◀ ◀ ◀

Detective: Arrest that mummy and bring me his wrap sheet.

▶ ▶ ▶ ▶ ▶ ▶ ▶ ▶ ▶ ▶ ▶ ▶ ▶ ▶ ▶ ▶ ▶ ▶ ▶ ▶

Monster Hunter #1: I'm going to follow these Sasquatch tracks.
Monster Hunter #2: Be careful. That's a big step you're taking.

◀ ◀ ◀ ◀ ◀ ◀ ◀ ◀ ◀ ◀ ◀ ◀ ◀ ◀ ◀ ◀ ◀ ◀ ◀ ◀

Knock! Knock!
Who's there?
Value.
Value who?
Value stop growling at me already.

What do you get if you cross a dinosaur with a witch's spell?
Tyrannosaurus Hex.

▶ ▶ ▶ ▶ ▶ ▶ ▶ ▶ ▶ ▶ ▶ ▶

Knock! Knock!
Who's there?
Uriah.
Uriah who?
Uriah is kind of red, Mr. Cyclops.

◀ ◀ ◀ ◀ ◀ ◀ ◀ ◀ ◀ ◀ ◀

Knock! Knock!
Who's there?
Thumb.
Thumb who?
Thumb folks like horror movies. I don't.

▶ ▶ ▶ ▶ ▶ ▶ ▶ ▶ ▶ ▶ ▶ ▶ ▶ ▶ ▶ ▶ ▶

Why are you at the hospital?
Vampire: I need a blood transfusion.
Mr. Zombie: I'm stiff all over.
Mr. Skeleton: I have a fractured bone.
The Invisible Man: I need to clear up my complexion.
Mrs. Devil: I'm having hot flashes.
Abominable Snowman: I have cold feet.
Werewolf: I'm shedding.
Ms. Witch: I'm having fainting spells.

◀ ◀ ◀ ◀ ◀ ◀ ◀ ◀ ◀ ◀ ◀ ◀ ◀ ◀ ◀ ◀ ◀

Why is the Frankenstein Monster so well informed?
He's full of current events.

▶ ▶ ▶ ▶ ▶ ▶ ▶ ▶ ▶ ▶ ▶ ▶ ▶ ▶ ▶ ▶ ▶

Mad Doctor: **I want to dissect this bee monster.**
Igor: **I'll get the buzz saw.**

What did one invisible man say to the other invisible man?
So long, I won't be seeing you around.

what's scary, hairy, and slides down an icy slope real fast?
A yeti on a snowboard.

Igor: Doctor, how's it going?
Dr. Frankenstein: Sew far, sew good.

Robot Space Monster #1: **Never invade earth on Sunday. It's too dangerous.**
Robot Space Monster #2: **Why is that?**
Robot Space Monster #1: **Because Sunday is a day of rust.**

ATTENTION: Bambi the Ghost is a deer haunter.

Vampire: What kind of mouthwash do you use?
Witch: Brand Hex.

How do you unlock a haunted house?
Use a skeleton key.

How did the fortune teller predict the monster's future?
She checked his horrorscope.

What did the Egyptian mummy say to the river?
Nile see you later.

Mad Doctor: Success at last! My apple monster is alive and it's rotten to the core!

Divorce Lawyer: Why are you here, Mrs. Frankenstein?

Mrs. Frankenstein: My marriage to the Mad Doctor was an experiment that failed.

High Priest: My mummy is always hungry.

Pharaoh: Maybe it has a tape worm.

Ivan: Want to hear a hangman's joke?

Igor: No. I don't care for gallows humor.

What do you get if you cross Big Foot with a space monster?

Huge star tracks.

Igor: Doctor, you charged this monster with the wrong kind of electricity.

Mad Doctor: What do you mean?

Igor: This creature has a negative attitude.

What happens when Frankenstein owns a butcher shop and has the Wolfman for a customer?

Frankenstein meats the Wolfman.

FLASH: Ms. Godzilla wears fishnet stockings.

What does the Abominable Snowman get when he eats ice cream too fast?

Brain freeze.

Boris: I think the Loch Ness monster is a girl.

Igor: What makes you say that?

Boris: Everyone says it's a she-serpent.

What kind of music do space monsters like?

Moon rock.

. . . .

NOTICE: A space monster from the planet Saturn just landed on earth. Be careful or it'll ring your neck.

. . . .

Where did T-Rex spend his summer vacation?

At the dinoshore.

. . . .

What is the ghost anthem of America?

Three scares for the red, white, and boo.

. . . .

What goes to college in the Midwest and carries a lot of food?

The lunchbag of Notre Dame.

. . . .

THE TWO-HEADED MONSTER ...

... enjoyed talking to himself.

... did a double-take when someone yelled, Head's up!

... was an expert at double-talk.

. . . .

Knock! Knock!

Who's there?

I spider.

I spider who?

I spider sneaking around our secret laboratory.

. . . .

What is T-Rex's favorite game?

Swallow the leader.

. . . .

Why shouldn't a witch on a broomstick lose her temper?

She might fly off the handle.

Who checks haunted houses?
The building in-spectre.

What did the referee say before the monsters' boxing match?
May the best frighter win.

What do you get when a fire-breathing dragon devours a male deer?
Hart burn.

What should you do if a monster breaks down your front door?
Run out the back door.

What did Dr. Frankenstein say to the three-legged monster?
You've grown a foot since I last saw you.

What did Godzilla say when he saw the vegetable garden?
Oh boy! Squash farmers.

What did the friendly geek ghost say?
Don't be afraid of the dork.

Who won the skeleton beauty contest?
No body.

Igor: Is your new girlfriend pretty?
Boris: Well, kind of.
Igor: Is she ugly?
Boris: In a way.
Igor: Then I guess she's pretty ugly.

What do you find on the windows of a haunted house?
Shudders.

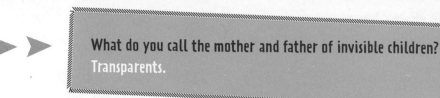

What do you call the mother and father of invisible children?
Transparents.

How do you make a skeleton laugh? Tickle its funny bone.

Why does the headless horseman ride every Halloween?
He's trying to get ahead in life.

What do you find on a haunted safari?
A big game haunter.

Who is the most famous witch detective?
Warlock Holmes.

Where do monsters like to water ski? On Lake Erie.

What is a ghost's favorite month?
Februscary.

Knock! Knock!
Who's there?
willis.
willis who?
willis nightmare ever end?

What do you do with a yellow monster?
Scare the big coward away.

Where do baby monsters stay while their parents work?
At dayscare centers.

Why are skeletons bad baseball players?
They make too many boneheaded plays.

What month was Frankenstein born?
Shocktober.

Igor: Is the Abominable Snowman a mean monster?
Boris: No, but he is a little cold-hearted.

Why did Frankenstein like to hear his Mad Doctor's jokes?
Because they kept him in stitches.

Drac: Does Mr. Skeleton play the trumpet?
Wolfie: No. He plays the trom-bone.

What do you do with a green monster? Let it ripen.

Boris: I know a monster with one eye called Cyclops.
Igor: What's his other eye called?

What skeleton was a famous music conductor?
Leonard Bonestein.

What do you call a skeleton that refuses to work?
Lazy bones.

What does a witch order while staying in a hotel?
Broom service.

Where do sea monsters sleep?
On waterbeds.

Witch: **Why did you give up fortune telling?**
Mystic: **I saw no future in it for me.**

What monster glows in the dark?
The Frankenshine Monster.

What did the witch say to her broom at bedtime?
Sweep dreams.

Zack: **Did you hear the latest monster joke?**
Jack: **Yes. It's a killer.**

What sound does a witch make when she cries?
Brew-hoo! Brew-hoo!

Why was the witch so thirsty?
She just had a dry spell.

What do you call two young witches who share
a dorm room?
Broom mates.

How do you make a haunted house more creepy?
Turn on the scare conditioner.

What did the Invisible Man say to his youngsters?
Children should be heard and not seen.

Why did Frankenstein act so goofy after meeting Dracula?
He was scared silly.

What did the evil mummy say after they wrapped him in aluminum?
Curses! Foiled again!

What's a cold evil candle called?
The Wicked Wick of the North.

What do you call a short play about witchcraft?
A magic act.

Why did the Mummy take a vacation?
He needed to unwind.

What did the little girl ghost get for her birthday?
A haunted dollhouse.

Why did the tidy witch put her broom in the washing machine?
She wanted to make a clean sweep.

What did the Mad Doctor say to his new monster?
You can be frank with me.

Why won't a witch wear a flat hat?
Because it's pointless.

▶ ▶ ▶ ▶ ▶ ▶ ▶ ▶ ▶ ▶ ▶ ▶ ▶ ▶ ▶ ▶ ▶

Why did the Hobbit have to stay after school?
He forgot to do his gnome work.

◀ ◀ ◀ ◀ ◀ ◀ ◀ ◀ ◀ ◀ ◀ ◀ ◀ ◀ ◀ ◀ ◀

What do you find at the top of Ghost Mountain?
Peak-a-boo.

▶ ▶ ▶ ▶ ▶ ▶ ▶ ▶ ▶ ▶ ▶ ▶ ▶ ▶ ▶ ▶ ▶

What kinds of football games do monsters like the best?
Ones that end in sudden-death overtime.

◀ ◀ ◀ ◀ ◀ ◀ ◀ ◀ ◀ ◀ ◀ ◀ ◀ ◀ ◀ ◀ ◀

Ghoul: did you like the horror movie?
Zombie: No. It bored me to death.

▶ ▶ ▶ ▶ ▶ ▶ ▶ ▶ ▶ ▶ ▶ ▶ ▶ ▶ ▶ ▶ ▶

Why do witches wear nametags at the Spelling Convention?
So they know which witch is which.

◀ ◀ ◀ ◀ ◀ ◀ ◀ ◀ ◀ ◀ ◀ ◀ ◀ ◀ ◀ ◀ ◀

Who does all of the talking at a ghost press conference?
The spooksperson.

▶ ▶ ▶ ▶ ▶ ▶ ▶ ▶ ▶ ▶ ▶ ▶

What is spookier than the outside of a haunted house?
The inside.

◀ ◀ ◀ ◀ ◀ ◀ ◀ ◀ ◀ ◀ ◀

What did the ghost order at the haunted Italian restaurant?
Spookgetti.

▶ ▶ ▶ ▶ ▶ ▶ ▶ ▶ ▶ ▶ ▶

What do you do with a blue monster?
Cheer it up.

About Applesauce Press

Good ideas ripen with time. From seed to harvest,
Applesauce Press crafts books with beautiful designs,
creative formats, and kid-friendly information on a variety
of fascinating topics. Like our parent company, Cider Mill Press
Book Publishers, our press bears fruit twice a year,
publishing a new crop of titles each spring and fall.

write to us at:
PO Box 454
12 Spring Street
Kennebunkport, ME 04046

Or visit us online at:
cidermillpress.com